# THE OFFICIAL
# POLITICALLY INCORRECT
# HANDBOOK
## Volume 2

**16 other books by the same authors (some of which are quite Politically Incorrect)**

The Complete Revenge Kit
How to be a Complete Bastard (with Adrian Edmondson)
How to be a Complete Bitch (with Pamela Stephenson)
The Book of Revelations
The Naughty 90s
The Return of the Complete Revenge Kit
How to be a Superhero
The Book of Stupid Lists
How to be a Real Man (with Julian Clary)
The Official Politically Incorrect Handbook – Volume 1
Back to Basics
The Ultimate Revenge Kit
Roy Chubby Brown Unzipped! (with Roy Chubby Brown)
The Office Revenge Kit
Rolf Harris's True Animal Tales (with Rolf Harris – naturally)
The Extra-terrestrial's Guide to the X-Files

# THE OFFICIAL POLITICALLY INCORRECT HANDBOOK
## Volume 2

Mark Leigh
and Mike Lepine

*Virgin*

First published in Great Britain in 1996 by
Virgin Books
an imprint of Virgin Publishing Ltd
332 Ladbroke Grove
London W10 5AH

A catalogue record for this book is available from the
British Library

ISBN 0-7535-0018-3

Typeset by Galleon Typesetting, Ipswich
Printed and bound in Great Britain by
Mackays of Chatham PLC

# Publisher's Apology

We're sorry. We really are. And we mean it. As some of you will know, we were conned into publishing Volume 1 of *The Official Politically Incorrect Handbook* in 1993. At the time, the authors' synopsis described the book as a collection of 'whimsically satirical observations about relationships and world politics'. We believed them and the result was a book that was in part or wholly responsible for the early reconvening of Parliament, 5,645 public order offences, a siege and an attempted coup (not to mention being the subject of the BBC current affairs documentary 'If this is free speech then let me live in Saudi Arabia').

Well, they've done it again. According to their contract we were committed to publishing a follow-up volume within four years. We tried to wriggle out of it but as well as threatening legal action 'which would bring the Virgin business empire to its very knees', they also had the negatives of our MD and that 'incident' at our 1995 office trip to London Zoo.

What can we say, then, apart from 'here it is' – and that we apologise if anyone is offended by the contents. We should point out that the views expressed by the authors herein are not necessarily those of Virgin Publishing or its employees (well, some of them, anyway) or agents.

Please, please don't write in and tell us how much you enjoyed it – it will only encourage them.

We've said it
before and we'll
say it again . . .

Many a true word is
spoken in jest

## ACID RAIN – Why it's a blessing in disguise

- It's the only thing that'll ever get our pavements clean
- If you leave your HP2 batteries out in it, you can extend their working lives up to 50%
- It kills Norwegian forests – which serves them right for all the whales
- It helps neutralise all the piss in our drinking water
- In 2,000 years time the hideous Pompidou Centre will have been reduced to a puddle
- Given a high enough concentration it will make the homeless problem disappear

## AESOP – 19 Politically Incorrect fables that he should have written

- The Hare and the Lapdancer
- The Lion and the Short Fat Ugly Bald Man
- The Sheep and the Welshman
- The Cow and the Abattoir
- The Fox and Prince Charles
- The Ant and the CFCs
- The Sly Wolf and the Bully

1

- The Old Weasel and the Joyrider
- The Trusting Calf and the Crafty Slaughterman
- The Happy Badger and the Bloke with the Smoke Canister
- The Goat and the Gestapo
- The Slow Cat and the Volvo
- The Elephant and the Landmine
- The Pig and the Hillbilly
- The Crow and the Lethal Injection
- The Horse and the Atomic Bomb
- The Gullible Whale and the Norwegian
- The Monkey and the Electrode
- The Eagle and the Egg Collector

## AFRICA – What it's good for

- Women who go around with their tits hanging out
- The title of a crappy song by Toto
- Ivory
- Pelts
- Rhino horns and other so-called aphrodisiacs for gullible Chinamen with two-inch dicks
- Nations so corrupt they make South American regimes look like the Brady Bunch
- Women with giraffe necks (the Dark Continent's version of 'pencil-necked geeks')
- Arms sales
- Padding out the Commonwealth
- Filling the bit between South America and India
- Misshapen bits of wood laughingly called 'crafts'
- Tarzan movies
- Dumping cigarettes and pharmaceuticals that kill people in the Western world
- The Ebola virus
- Delicacies involving ants and dung
- An excuse for saving up old milk bottle tops and sending them to *Blue Peter*
- Making you feel better about living in Peckham
- Calling it 'Bongo Bongo' Land

## AGONY AUNTS – Some Politically Incorrect things for them to do

- Print the reader's full name and postal address
- Make up some really vile and incriminating letters from people they hate and print *their* full name and postal address
- Have a good laugh in the office at someone's expense (then throw their letter in the bin)
- Promote unsafe sex
- Give completely the wrong advice then sit back with a chocolate flake and imagine the terrible consequences
- Make readers feel insecure by 'revealing' that the average penis length is 10½ inches (and larger when erect), any woman that can't reach orgasm has deep-rooted lesbian tendencies, and that most couples do it five times a night (more at weekends)
- Forward letters on to the police
- Or partners
- Have a special section in their column called 'Loser of the Week'
- Blackmail readers who have particularly juicy problems/admissions

## ALCOHOLIC LEMONADE – 13 other products that should be targeted at the young

- Brandy Sherbet Dib Dabs
- Vodka 'n' Vinegar Crisps
- Pic 'n' Mix Hair of the Dog
- Guinness Gobstoppers
- Harvey Wallbanger Liquorice Allsorts
- Jelly Baby Liqueurs
- Dolly Mixture Chasers
- Acid Drop Aperitifs
- Castlemaine XXXX Lucky Bags
- Burgundy Bubble Gum
- Beaujolais Nouveau Wine Gums

- Martini Rusks
- Teething rings that taste of cognac

## ALIEN ABDUCTIONS – Why the 'Greys' never abduct the Welsh

- They put too great a power drain on the brain probe
- Before the aliens can conduct their usual rectal examination, they have to prise the leek out
- They tread sheep turds in with them and the flying saucer stinks for weeks afterwards
- Half the time, the aliens can't be sure if they're abducting a man or a woman
- If you kidnap more than one, they start singing
- Welsh-speakers sound like the dreaded Reptile Men of Deneb IV (with head colds)
- They're a particularly violent race. Ask them their names and they just scowl 'die!' – which is very intimidating if you're only three feet tall
- It takes forever to get the wool out of their semen-suctioning devices
- It takes half an hour to peel their underpants off because they haven't changed them since Wales were last in the World Cup
- The aliens want to improve their genetic stock, not degrade it

## ALLIGATOR WRESTLING – 10 similar demeaning (but nonetheless compelling) pastimes to take away animals' dignity

- Koala Sumo
- Llama Taekwondo
- Tortoise Kickboxing
- Giant Panda Ju-Jitsu
- Thomson's Gazelle Aikido
- Pelican Karate
- Peacock Bare Knuckle Fighting
- Carp Kendo

- Giraffe Judo
- Donkey Hitting in the Bollocks with a Cricket Bat

## ALTERNATIVE RELIGIONS – Why it's a good thing to learn about them in schools

- So we know we're not missing anything
- They're a good laugh
- We can sneer at beliefs even more stupid and far-fetched than our own
- They help us to lose respect for others who really don't deserve it
- We can tease people of different religions with some degree of accuracy
- You can ask to be excused from the lesson
- Suddenly, your own personal religion doesn't seem half so loopy
- You can ask your teacher embarrassing questions about female circumcision and sexual equality
- Or why God wants women to put a sack over their heads
- They help you to understand why 50 million people in the Middle East all personally hate your guts and want to see you dead
- Other people's hymns and chants are often hilarious
- Understanding a person's religion helps you to understand why his country is so shitty

## AMNESTY INTERNATIONAL – Why it should mind its own damn business

- None of the people they harp on about have actually been given an amnesty
- Some people actually like being tortured and pay good money to be flogged within an inch of their life
- It's only thanks to the Secret Police that there isn't total anarchy in Brazil

- Not everyone wants to watch *The Secret Policeman's Ball*
- Most of the people wanting 'political asylum' just want to get into our country and bum off our welfare state
- With all the cows being incinerated, we have to look to Saudi Arabia to take all the cattle prods off our hands
- Who takes any notice of the UN's declaration of human rights anyway?
- If authors suffer revolting brutality it will give them another experience to write about (political dissident writing never flourishes under a liberal regime)
- Indeed, if it hadn't been for political repression, Solzhenitsyn would never have written *The Gulag Archipelago* – instead he would have penned *Confessions of a Siberian Love Vixen*
- If Amnesty ever manage to get every prisoner of conscience released they won't have anything left to do
- Exporting torture implements helps keep Britain's economy in the black
- If we couldn't sell these things to the South Americans, Europe would be faced with a thumb screw mountain
- If the Brazilian police can't abduct street children and steal their vital organs, thousands of innocent, rich elderly Americans will die
- Do the Chilean death squads tell Amnesty International how to run *their* business?

**ANCIENT EGYPTIANS – Why they were a bunch of tossers and not a highly civilised race**

- They worshipped cats
- And scarab beetles
- Even a jackal-headed man
- They could only draw people sideways

- They walked in a silly way
- They married their brothers and sisters . . .
- . . . or in many cases themselves
- Their tomb houses were called 'mastabas' – which sounds a bit rude
- They built huge great pyramids just because they couldn't be arsed to buy new razor blades
- They used pictures instead of letters so it took 20 minutes just to draw a note for the milkman
- They wrapped up their dead in bandages – even though it was too late to make them better
- They prepared their dead for their new life by pulling their brains out through their noses
- Whenever one of them comes back to life in a movie he always gets destroyed really easily
- They laboured for centuries to create the Riddle of the Sphinx when they could just as easily have left posterity a crossword puzzle
- They believed that it was safe to cross the Red Sea

## PAMELA ANDERSON – Why the US Government should make her their Foreign Secretary

- Iraqi leaders would be so distracted by her cleavage that they'd fail to stop a UN resolution being passed which upheld sanctions against them
- If there was a Nobel Prize given for Foreign Secretaries Posing Naked, she'd win hands down, miles ahead of even Malcolm Rifkind
- She'd have the biggest breasts of any postwar American Foreign Secretary – with the obvious exception of Henry 'Chesty' Kissinger
- If there was a dispute between China and Tibet over political control of the Himalayas, her tits and a felt pen could be used to demonstrate the disputed borders
- Because of an intense personal interest, she'd be ideal when it came to negotiating over a threatened embargo of silicon shipments

- She could help sustain world peace by offering foreign leaders a blow-job in exchange for a ceasefire (a ploy not seriously considered by Lord Owen or Cyrus Vance – although Douglas Hurd once settled a fishing dispute with a timely hand shandy)
- She would be ideally placed for sensitive Middle East peace negotiations because she could consult with her good friend David Hasselhoff who's Jewish (or if he's not, he sounds like he could be)
- If Yasser Arafat accidentally fell into the Red Sea, she could use her *Baywatch* lifesaving skills to rescue him
- She'd be a good role model for girls wishing to take up a career in politics

## ANIMAL TESTING – Things we should test on animals, *just in case* we ever need them

- Cough sweets with a boiling oil centre
- A DIY home spontaneous combustion kit
- A pregnancy testing kit that shoots barbed spikes out everywhere
- A Semtex suppository
- An electrified bagel
- Red-hot pokers
- Toothpaste with extra hydrochloric acid
- A microwave that cooks everything *outside* itself
- An amateur eye removal device
- A sandwich toaster-cum-cock guillotine
- Pasta shapes that give you instantaneous renal failure
- A door that opens on to a long drop
- Yet another shampoo

## ANIMAL TESTING – Why it's good for them

- It's a steady job
- It's a regular job until they die

- They get free meals (all right, so the meal may be laced with major carcinogens – but then, so are most human meals)
- Completing a maze gives them a sense of personal achievement
- If you're a rat who's into body piercing, this just might be your dream come true!
- There are lots of doctors about to take care of them
- Kind people take them out of their cages and handle them
- All the other lab animals respect you when you become the first mouse in history to grow a human ear out of your khyber
- The lab is nice and warm (unless they're taking part in a freezing experiment, of course)
- All the shampoo tipped over them helps keep their fur in tip-top condition
- They're treated better than they would be as a pet on many council estates

## ANOREXICS – Some particularly unhelpful things to say to them

- Hiya, fatty!
- Hey, Mama Cass! I thought you were dead . . .
- Who's my little chubby-chops, then?
- Bet you can't resist this delicious piece of fudge cake; bet you . . .
- Gosh. Kate Moss! You've filled out since I last saw you
- Hey, looking good!
- Well, they do say, you can't be too rich or too thin . . .
- If I thought about all the shit they put in our food nowadays, I'd be an anorexic too
- Cor! Lose a few more pounds and you could be a supermodel!
- You've put on weight! Great, you've finally beaten your problem!

- Would you like to try this new slimming product?
- When's the baby due?
- Live fast, die young, leave a good-looking corpse! That's the motto for today . . .

## THE ARMY – Why the government should spend money recruiting soldiers rather than doctors and nurses

- To get a lot of deeply stupid (and completely unemployable) school leavers off the dole
- A battalion of Green Jackets could storm an enemy pillbox with ease. A team of consultant anaesthetists would be cut to ribbons in no time
- The Queen would soon get very bored with inspecting a line-up of ear, nose and throat consultants
- To provide welcome support for the Cypriot pub and bar industry
- However skilled, a junior doctor would be absolutely useless trying to drive a Challenger tank over rocky terrain (especially after 72 hours without sleep)
- A foreign embassy is more likely to be successfully stormed by the SAS than the NHS
- Tourists would not flock to see the Changing of the Dressing (and if they did, would probably say 'Yuk!' and have to look away)
- A country that relies on urologists as a last line of defence will soon be overrun
- Although good with their hands, no gynaecologist could strip down and reassemble an Armalite rifle in under 90 seconds
- Who wants to watch a march-by by the massed bands of the Junior Radiographers?
- Anyone wearing a white coat in the middle of a battle would be a sitting duck (unless, it must be said, they happen to be fighting in the Arctic Circle)

- A staff sergeant is trained to kill a man. A staff nurse is only trained to save one

## ART, MODERN – Why it's rubbish

- You can't tell what it's meant to be
- A bunch of squiggles is still a bunch of squiggles, no matter how much the Tate offers for it
- Stuffing a potato up your arse and sitting in a glass display case is a cry for help, not an expression of artistic temperament
- Anything that looks better to you drunk than sober has to be suspect
- Sliced cows belong in an abattoir (or, more recently, in an incinerator), not in an art gallery
- A brick is a brick; any five-year-old can tell you that
- Two pieces of corrugated steel sheeting and a length of rubber hose do not represent man's alienation in a godless universe. They don't, they just don't
- How can you objectively decide that a green splodge is better than a purple smear?
- When a 'tactile creation' called 'Adam and Eve' looks like a car wreck, something's wrong somewhere
- A dead sheep is a kebab, not an *objet d'art*
- I could do that – with my eyes closed

## ART, SURREALIST – Why it's rubbish

- Fish

## BABE – Politically Incorrect things to think about while watching the movie

- Chops
- Sizzling bacon in the pan
- A packet of pork scratchings
- Old girlfriends
- That scene from *Deliverance*
- The Torah
- Pigskin handbags and matching shoes
- A porcine dildo
- Unsuccessful high altitude attempts to prove the scientific proposition that 'Pigs might fly'
- *The Bill*
- Babe's uncanny resemblance to Tony Blair
- Sex
- Kinky piglet-sized silk undies and matching basque
- What they did with the piglet afterwards

## BADGER-BAITING – Some alliterative alternatives for those jaded with the usual form of the sport

- Badger-bayoneting
- Badger-bashing

- Badger-bludgeoning
- Badger-bazooka-ing
- Badger-bisecting
- Badger-beating
- Badger-bollock blending
- Badger-blowing up
- Badger-biffing
- Badger-braising
- Badger-belting
- Badger-boxing
- Badger-buggering

## BADGER-BAITING – Some non-alliterative but still nonetheless amusing alternatives for the *really* jaded blood sports enthusiasts

- Badger-harpooning
- Badger-nuking
- Badger-flamethrowering
- Badger-napalming
- Badger-machete-ing
- Badger-armour-piercing missiling
- Badger-running over with the XR3i
- Badger-kidney punching
- Badger-headbutting
- Badger-surface-to-air-missile up the jacksie-ing

## BAG LADIES – Things you do want to hear them say

- Remember me? I used to teach you chemistry
- Remember me? I turned you down for a loan at the building society
- Remember me? I turned you down for a dance at the sixth-form disco
- I knew I shouldn't have jilted you at the altar
- It's strange but true – laughing at the size of your thing was the start of my downfall . . .
- Yes, I did use to be your boss. Funny old world, innit?

- You were drunk, but I wouldn't let you do nothing . . .
- Remember me? I used to be Prime Minister

## BAG LADIES – Things you wouldn't want to hear them say to you

- Fancy a snog, sonny?
- I'm your blind date
- Only £1 to sniff me armpits. Go on, be a devil!
- You were so drunk, you didn't care where you put it . . .
- I had the same pension plan as you
- Ta-da! Septicaemia!
- I'm you, sonny, come back from the future to warn you not to mess with your gender alignment . . .
- Yes, I took your wallet. It's down my gusset
- Hello, son. How's your dad?

## BEAGLES – 10 things they should test on them apart from cigarettes

- Ten-ton weights
- The effects of 122G
- Cruise missiles
- Anything that affects their immune system
- Rusty man-traps
- Barbed wire
- Pneumatic jack-hammers
- Concentrated hydrofluoric acid
- Chieftain tanks
- Cigars

## BEATITUDES – The more honest ones the Bible left out

- Blessed are the mighty, for they can duff up the meek
- Blessed are those with rich parents
- Blessed are those who don't look like the back end of oxen

- Blessed are the big nobs, for obvious reasons
- Blessed is the Messiah who happens to be omnipresent, even though girls' shower rooms have yet to be invented
- Blessed are the children, for they do not yet know how crappy life is
- Blessed are those that can afford to change their chariot every August
- Blessed are local councillors; for they have a cushy number

## BEEF – Why you should feed your children British beef

- It's pretty cheap right now
- You hate them
- The shop was all out of rat poison
- Culinary Russian Roulette gives you a perverse thrill
- They're brighter than you are and you feel threatened
- They're brighter than you are and you don't know any better
- If you don't fuck their brains up, the schooling system will only do it anyway
- You've eaten so much beef that you always believe what the Tories tell you
- You've eaten so much beef that . . . wibble, wibble, hatstand
- You're a member of the Cabinet and the British farming lobby is more important than your daughter's life

## BEEF, BRITISH – 10 things that are probably far safer

- Brazilian spiders
- American serial killers
- South African townships
- Italian politics
- Russian mafiosi
- African diseases

- Indian drinking water
- Egyptian bottled water
- French nuclear testing
- Colombian drug barons

## BETTING – Why it's good to encourage kids to gamble

- You can win their pocket money back off them in a game of three-card stud
- Projecting a return from the odds helps them with their maths
- It's also a fun way to learn about the various theories of probability
- It's preferable for kids to supplement their pocket money from gambling than from drug dealing
- Or theft
- Or extortion
- They'll have something in common with 80% of their parents
- How else can you turn a week's dinner money into £200?
- If they're gambling they're not joyriding
- Or masturbating over pictures of Louise in a well-used copy of *Smash Hits*
- If they grow up to be James Bond they can put Scaramanga to shame in the casino – and steal his bird
- You can have a man-to-man talk with your son – and exchange racing tips
- They'll understand how to put a triple accumulator bet on for you – without you having to get off the sofa
- So you don't have to go to Gamblers Anonymous on your own

## THE BIBLE – 14 new New Testament books to make the Bible popular once more

- The Book of the Barbie Twins
- The Book of Monster Trucks

- The Book of Breast Augmentation
- The Book of Big Guns
- The Book of Red Hot Saucy Bi-Girl Stories
- The Book of Free Tesco Vouchers
- The Book of Numbers (winning lottery ones, that is)
- The Book of Judges (who died slowly and messily in their own viscera)
- The Book of Readers' Wives
- The Book of Sex Acts of the Apostles
- The Book of Ten First-Class Stamps
- The Book of Revelations (about Hollywood's top sex symbols)
- The Book of Tickets for Chessington World of Adventures
- The Book of the Film

## BIG ARNIE – Catchphrases he'd be better off avoiding – or not stealing

- I'm free, asshole!
- Oooh, no, missus asshole!
- I'll be back – in a dress, asshole!
- I can suck golf balls through a hosepipe, asshole!
- *Hasta la vista*, big boy!
- My panties are bunching, asshole!
- Shut that door . . . asshole!
- Rock on, asshole!
- Look at the muck in here, asshole!
- Bottle, glass . . . glass, bottle, asshole!
- 'Allo, playmates – oh, I mean assholes!

## BIG ARNIE – *Dad's Army* catchphrases he'd be better off avoiding

- Don't panic, asshole!
- Put that light out, asshole!
- We're doomed, asshole!
- Uncle Arthur, Uncle Arthur, asshole!

- Stupid boy – asshole!
- They don't like it up their assholes!

## THE BIG ISSUE – 2 things it's far better to spend 70p on

- Yourself
- Anything else

## THE BIG ISSUE – Why it's bollocks

- It's sold by some smelly, dishevelled oik in filthy clothes rather than a pert young sixteen-year-old shop assistant you can chat up
- The vendors pocket some of the money you pay for it; if Martin's or W. H. Smith's staff tried that, they'd be out on their ear in no time
- The ads are all for free legal advice and temporary accommodation – something that's only relevant to the dosser selling it
- The features are all about things like the Mental Health Act or the new Asylum Bill, not a profile of Claudia Schiffer or a comparative test on six sports coupés
- There're no colour photos of scantily clad babes you can fantasise about; just some grainy black-and-white pics of people who've run away from home
- The problem pages are filled with stuff about claiming benefits and being hassled by the police – nothing relevant to your life like not achieving a viable erection or wanting to wear women's clothing
- There're no photos of celebrities snapped as they enter/leave posh restaurants or nightclubs
- Or showbiz gossip
- The magazine smells funny because last night the dosser stuffed it down his underpants to keep him warm
- You'll never, ever, ever need to know where and when John Hegley is in concert

18

- Or where you can apply for a job as a 'Literary Support Tutor'
- Or a 'Qualified Auricular Acupuncturist'
- You're frightened of catching something from it
- With an average page count of just 44, it's questionable whether the magazine can be justified as 'Big'
- After you tear it into strips, the print comes off on your bum

## TONY BLAIR – What's he hiding? Some guesses

- Three nipples
- A large 666 birthmark on his scalp
- A collection of ties from the 1970s
- A completely empty scrotal sac
- A love letter from Michael Barrymore
- A passion for the blonde one in Abba
- His brief and glorious career as ship's pin-up on HMS *Brigantine*
- The fact that he's Ronnie Corbett's love child
- A cupboard full of XXXX-strength testosterone supplements that didn't work
- Reds under the bed
- Huge tax rises

## BLIND PEOPLE – Things to do behind their backs to upset them

- Anything you bloody like, as long as you're quiet

## BLOODY SUNDAY – 6 other days in the Irish calendar that are far worse

- Piss Awful Friday
- Fucking Thursday
- Bastard Monday
- Shitty Saturday
- Crappy Wednesday
- Load of Old Bollocks Tuesday

## THE BOAT PEOPLE – How we should deal with them

- Direct all the oil supertankers with pissed captains into their vicinity
- Send Navy frogmen to sneak on board and switch their compasses around 180 degrees when no one's looking
- Tell those interned in Hong Kong that they're off for a free trip to Disneyland (not mentioning that short stopover in Ho Chi Minh City)
- Invite them all to come and live in England (they'll soon want to go back)
- Send naval coastguard ships to sail alongside them, loudspeakers blaring out 'Greasy bacon! Fried eggs! Fried bread!' until everyone on board feels so seasick they demand to return to port
- Offer to exchange their crappy old junks for our nice safe cross-Channel ferries
- Set up giant fans on the shores of Hong Kong to blow them back where they came from
- Offer guided tours of the camps to crazed Vietnam vets who 'wanna win, this time'
- Invite the American Navy to attack all the military shipping in the area (that way, they're bound to sink all the boat people in unfortunate 'friendly fire' incidents)
- Pretend they're all going to be used as well-paid extras in *Apocalypse Now 2*. Only reveal on the boat that, for extra realism, the epic will be filmed in Vietnam . . .
- Continue on just the way we are – until the international community gets so outraged by our human rights abuses that they take them off our hands

## BODY PIERCING – Why it's the act of a moron and not a fashion statement

- A nose stud looks remarkably like a huge wart
- Or a stray, northward-bound bogie

20

- It is not manly to be led around on a chain attached to rings sunk through your nipples
- Contrary to what they tell you, having a glans stud put in hurts like all fuck
- Your tongue stud could get caught in your teeth brace. You'd end up talking like the Elephant Man and no one would understand what was wrong with you
- A tongue stud weeping with pus does *not* enhance fellatio
- If you go near a powerful magnet, you could get trapped
- Only girls as disfigured as you are will fancy you
- If you wear rings through your eyebrows, you're just crying out for someone to thread curtains through them and pull them shut
- Gypsies might mug you for all the scrap metal
- Supposing your Prince Albert (your foreskin ring) gets caught in her clitoris stud? The Fire Brigade will have to come out with arc-welding gear to cut you free
- If you wear nylon underpants, your testicle rings will keep giving you violent electric shocks
- Imagine the embarrassment of setting off the metal detectors at the airport and having to show the security staff your foreskin rings
- If you want to make a hole in your head, do everyone a favour and use a .44

## BORN AGAIN CHRISTIANS – They might have found Jesus but what's still missing from their sad lives?

- An original thought
- A grasp of the fact that corduroy and opened-toed sandals make them look like King Dick
- The realisation that nobody gives a toss when they stand in the streets and shout at passers-by
- Friends

- Free will
- A sense of humour
- A sense of reality
- The 'other' Good Book (the one with all the naked pictures of Madonna in)
- A grip
- Hot 'n' horny sex

## BOTTLE BANKS – Why they're a complete waste of time

- You can't chat up the cashiers
- They're more difficult to break into than your local Barclays or NatWest
- And if you did manage to break in, it's hard to make a quick getaway with a sack full of broken glass
- You can't go into them and pretend you're interested in a mortgage, just to get out of the rain and get a free cuppa
- You can't nick the stubby little pens on chains
- They won't issue a statement telling you how many bottles you've just deposited
- If you want to withdraw your bottles late at night it's almost impossible
- You don't get a £10 Pizzaland voucher when you open an account
- They're not in the high street but always somewhere you never go (like outside the local library or in the B&Q car park)
- They don't offer telebanking facilities so you can't phone them at 9.30 at night (unless you're mental)
- Their rate of interest is crap – even worse than a high-street bank

## BOXING HELENA – Other methods of packaging women in the tradition of this sexist masterpiece

- Sealing Up Cecilia
- Crating Clarissa
- Packaging Petulia
- Wrapping Up Rita
- Gift-Wrapping Gail
- Parcelling Pauline
- Cartoning Carla
- Casing Cora
- Containing Candy
- Kitbagging Katy
- Stowing Stella
- Stashing Stephanie
- Encasing Edna
- Framing Felicity
- Penning Penelope
- Encompassing Emma
- Enfolding Ermintrude
- Sheathing Sharon

## BOYS' SCHOOLS – Why single-sex schools are much better than mixed

- There are no girls in your class undergoing puberty who might take your mind off studying
- There's very little chance of you catching VD before you leave
- It doesn't matter if you get really spotty because there are no girls to see you and laugh
- There's no school disco so you won't be embarrassed about not having a date
- You're far more likely to join the chess club in a single-sex school
- Plain and dumpy women teachers feel good because they know 500 boys have a crush on them
- You're more likely to come home with a good report than love-bites
- You can explore your feminine side when you're asked to play Yum-Yum in the all-boy school's version of *The Mikado*
- You won't have a rival to the girl you fancy
- You won't have to spend all your day planning how to 'accidentally' bump into her as she walks to the bus-stop
- You won't feel embarrassed learning about the facts of life in biology rather than the bike shed

23

- If you're really ugly you'll have a few years of grace before discovering what rejection is all about
- You find out that there *is* a joyous alternative to heterosexuality

## BREAST AUGMENTATION – Why the NHS should fund this rather than organ transplants

- Girls have more confidence with a big chest than a big scar
- There are no complications after having your bosoms made bigger (apart from being ogled at by loads of men, which in itself is not life-threatening)
- Men can't put their faces between a new kidney and go 'blub, blub, blub, blub, blub' (well, they can, but it's rather messy, not to say completely unhygienic)
- If a breast enlargement goes wrong you can just do it again; try doing that with open heart surgery
- A new lung does not make a girl more sexually attractive – no matter how big it is
- *Penthouse* has not (to the best of our knowledge) published features such as 'Readers' Wives with New Livers'
- Or 'Kinky Kidneys!'
- Or 'Sexy Spleens!'
- Britain has yet to produce its answer to Pamela Anderson
- Big breasts are more of a sight for sore eyes than a new cornea
- Patients reject donor organs all the time: nobody ever rejects big tits

## BREAST ENLARGEMENTS – Why your wife/girlfriend should have them

- As a cunning play on the 'feel-good factor'
- So you'll hang around with her a bit longer
- You've invested your life savings in silicon futures

- Your mates will all be jealous
- So you can tell her apart from her brother
- So you can pretend that she's Pamela Anderson when the lights go out
- So that you might get an erection once more
- So that *Razzle* Readers' Wives page won't keep sending her picture back with the terse note 'Don't fancy yours, mate'
- So she can win lots of 'Wet T-Shirt' contests the length and breadth of the Costa del Sol
- For the good of the nation
- So another bloke will take her off your hands

## THE BRITISH EMPIRE – Why it was such a spiffing idea

- Maps looked so much prettier covered in all that pink
- Without it, half of the valuable stamps in the authors' collections just wouldn't exist
- Decimating Zulus gave British soldiers invaluable practice for the First World War
- Being decimated by the Zulus in turn also gave British soldiers invaluable practice for the First World War
- The Empire gave us somewhere to dump all our criminals and religious nutters
- If the Empire had never existed, the Queen wouldn't be able to give MBEs and OBEs to so many deserving people like lollipop ladies and has-been actors
- If the Empire had never existed, The Empire, Leicester Square, might have been called the Odeon and become confused with the other Odeon in the Square, thus upsetting many a moviegoer
- It inspired such great films as *Carry On up the Khyber*
- The English language is so much richer for the multitude of racial insults and slurs it inspired

- It enables the Queen to go to loads of tossy countries she would otherwise not have an excuse to visit

## BRITISH FILMS – Why they're crap

- Where are all the car chases in *Pride and Prejudice*?
- Peter Greenaway couldn't direct a shoot-'em-up if his life depended on it
- They have Arnold Schwarzennegger, we have Stephen Fry
- We make films based on Thomas Hardy, they have films based on Tom Clancy
- Mike Leigh films are desperately short of amazing stunts
- If John Woo directed *Trainspotting*, it would be ten times as good
- You just know that, if the British made *9½ Weeks*, it would be about two deeply alienated homosexual working-class trainee hairdressers from Camden
- You just know that if the British made *Jurassic Park*, it would be about two deeply alienated homosexual trainee hairdressers from Camden
- It's hard to make a good film with just £40,000 and a mate who can borrow a camera

## BRUSSELS – What you need to be elected to the EU

- A snout for the prime trough
- Friends in the One World conspiracy
- A very silly accent (see, it's even true for Kinnock)
- A distinct absence of patriotism (see, it's even true for Kinnock)
- A two-inch dick (see, it's even true for Kinnock)
- A hatred of everything British
- Six votes at most (because hardly anyone bothers to vote in European elections)

## BUDDHISM – Why it never caught on over here

- Fat bald blokes aren't very appealing in the West – there're just too many of them
- Buddha is a silly name
- Buddha was a prince, and we know better than to respect royalty
- Living again and again in Britain is a worse fate than going to hell
- The songs aren't catchy enough
- Meditation is boring
- Wearing saffron robes doesn't attract the chicks
- A disinterest in money isn't merely strange, it's pathological
- We don't like to venerate our ancestors – we prefer to stick them in a council home and visit them once a year
- Vegetarian food tastes like shit
- Britons aren't interested in reaching Nirvana. They're happy if they make it to Malaga once a year

## BULIMIA – Why sufferers are such lucky bastards

- They can stuff themselves stupid with Mars Bars and still not gain weight
- They can throw up without having to spend a fortune on drink first
- They can get a job testing airline sick-bags
- Or the stain resistance of minicab seat covers
- It's one of the few diets that actually work
- If they meet Princess Di at a party they immediately have something in common
- Hardly anyone else has the nickname 'Vomo'
- If they study fine art they have loads of opportunities to examine porcelain close up
- It's better than being really anorexic
- Or really, really fat

## BULIMICS – How you can help them

- Stick two fingers down their throats for them
- Punch them hard and unexpectedly in the lower abdomen
- Keep lifting up the cat's tail to reveal its bum to them
- Eat huge gobfuls of food with your mouth open right in front of them
- Be violently sick right in front of them
- Turn your underpants inside out and show them the state of them
- Offer them £10 every time they blow chunks as a positive incentive
- Tread dog pooh into the carpet and let them clean it up
- Make them eat everything that's found down the back of the sofa
- Shoot them and put them out of their misery

## BULLYING – 15 helpful things to say to children who complain about it

- When I was your age . . . (followed by any old crap)
- If you don't like the heat, stay out of the kitchen
- It's character-building
- Stop whinging
- Well, son, it's a dog-eat-dog world out there
- Pull yourself together!
- Hospital food is much better than it used to be
- Go bother Esther Rantzen, I'm watching telly . . .
- Serves you right for having a stutter!
- Serves you right for being able to read!
- You probably asked for it
- Crybaby!
- If anyone asks, I didn't give you this Stanley knife . . .
- Haven't you heard of the survival of the fittest?

- Go up to your room – and if I come up there in fifteen minutes, I don't want to find you hanging dead in your wardrobe!

## BUREAUCRATS – Things EU bureaucrats do not possess

- A heart
- A soul
- A 32-inch waist
- A penis that would satisfy a small rodent
- Any idea whatsoever of what they are talking about
- Your best interests at heart

## BUREAUCRATS – Things EU bureaucrats do possess

- Front
- Bias
- A large plastic vibrating thing for stimulating even the most jaded of prostates
- The ability to do exactly the wrong thing at the wrong time
- A seventeen-year-old mistress in a flat paid for by Brussels
- A 'friend' named Sasha to tighten the nipple clamps
- A large complimentary car ideal for cruising for boys
- A plastic bag, a length of cord, an orange – and a 10 × 8 of Julio Iglesias
- Several Swiss bank accounts for 'consultation fees' and 'gratuities'
- Satan's unlisted home phone number
- 24-hour access to the EU champagne mountain
- The ability to play Babe's dad in the sequel
- You and me

## BUTCHER'S ASSISTANT – Why it's good to be one

- It's easy to get a job (they can't be fussy who they take on)
- When you take the cleaver to a carcass, you can pretend it's the boss
- You have access to all sorts of sharp cutting and chopping tools . . .
- You can faithfully recreate that famous scene in *Alien* by flinging offal all over the shop
- You can have 'custard pie' fights with lumps of raw liver
- You can hollow out a pig's head, put it over your own and then serve the customers
- You can have sex with a plucked chicken in the cold store and pretend it's Sharon Stone
- You can have sex with a whole pig's carcass round the back by the dustbins and pretend it's Dawn French
- You can masturbate in the storehouse and when the boss asks what you're doing you can say, 'Just beating the meat' – and you'll be telling the truth
- You can strut around with a prime pork sausage sticking out of your flies in front of all the housewives
- You can play 'dare' with your winkie and the bacon slicer
- You can play 'certain screaming agony' with your winkie and a bacon slicer
- At the end of the day, you can chase vegetarians down the street with your bloody apron

## CALVES – Why they don't really mind being cooped up in veal crates

- They don't wear themselves out wandering around
- For a newly born calf, it's a very comforting 'back to the womb' experience
- The confinement focuses their minds so they can take in every memorable aspect of their journey
- At any given time they're never very far away from any of their calf friends
- Agoraphobic calves are exceptionally well catered for
- If the lorry goes over a bump, there's no chance of them falling over and hurting themselves
- They're preferable to the alternatives – 'Veal Tupperware Boxes' or 'Veal Plastic Dustbins'
- They know that there's a group of dedicated animal rights protesters fighting for their welfare; this wouldn't be the case if they were in 'Veal Spacious Pens' or 'Veal Luxury Apartments'

31

## CAMBODIA – The 13 most popular nicknames for landmine victims

- 'Hopalong'
- 'Wobbly'
- 'Limpy'
- 'Stumpy'
- 'Hobbler'
- 'Crawler'
- 'Crutch Boy'
- 'Lameo'
- 'Uni Lad'
- 'Shorty'
- 'Leggy'
- 'Mister No Legs'
- 'Slitherer'

## THE CAR – Why it's an absolute godsend

- It gives Aborigines somewhere to live
- It gives thick Dagenham men some hope of paid employment
- You can't have it off in the back of a moped
- It can give men hung like a chipmunk the feeling of being 'one of the big boys'
- It gives joyriders a way to kill themselves before they grow up to become major dangers to society
- Road-ragers would look silly on trikes
- Bruce Springsteen would have nothing to sing about
- Without Skoda jokes, the world would be a poorer place
- It gives Jeremy Clarkson a way to relieve his over-inflated libido
- It makes great screeching noises when you take corners too fast
- Have you tried travelling on public transport recently?
- If you kill someone with a knife, you get banged away for life, but if you kill someone with your car, you're out in a year – tops! It's the best way to murder someone there is!

## CAR ACCESSORIES – Some extras we'll soon need to deal with road-ragers

- Lucas Anti-Cut-You-Up .50-Calibre Brownings
- Halford's Cunt in a Van Car-to-Car Heat-Seeking Missiles
- Unipart Driving-up-Your-Backside Aft Incinerators
- Girling Git Who Flashes At You To Move Over For Him Rear-Mounted Rocket Pods
- Pirelli Tyre Scythes
- Kwik-Fit Bumper Bazookas
- Pifco Roof Rack with 75mm 'Nearside Overtaking' Cannon

## CARE – Things children can expect in council care today

- To meet a man with glassy eyes who makes them dress up as Lassie and force-feed him wine gums
- To meet all his friends
- To be on heroin by their thirteenth birthday
- To be on the game by their twelfth birthday
- To meet the future members of their mugging gang
- No one to be watching when they run away to London
- All the warning signs to be ignored
- To attend an inquiry ten years too late

## CARE – Things children can't expect in council care today

- Care

## CARE IN THE COMMUNITY – How to spot people on this scheme

- Their faces regularly appear on *Crime Monthly*
- Someone waving a carving knife and yelling 'I'm Jesus Christ' while wearing their underpants over

their head is more likely to be a Care in the Community patient than the Second Coming

- Cheese is rarely worn on the head by rational members of society
- It's not every day you see someone trying to bite through a bicycle
- God seldom tells his chosen to attempt to eat their own faeces
- They've broken into your house and are presently shagging your hi-fi
- They've climbed into your car at the traffic lights and want to discuss how aliens stole their socks
- Naked men singing 'We Are the World' and brandishing a shotgun are probably not street entertainers
- A 30-year-old man covered in warpaint running amok in Tesco's is another good bet
- They come out of secure facilities almost as soon as they're sent in
- The council wants to house them next door to you
- They're completely on their own

## CARE IN THE COMMUNITY – Some equally safe alternatives

- Giving a patient a handgun and saying, 'You see that bloke over there? He's Satan, he is . . .'
- Juggling three flame-throwers in a petrol station
- Trying to give a fully grown Bengal tiger a hand job
- Trying to give Mike Tyson a hand job
- Trying to stow away to America by hiding inside a Jumbo's engine
- Bungee-jumping without a rope
- Wife-swapping with O.J. Simpson
- Putting on a blond wig and going up to O.J.'s kitchen window saying, 'Whooooooo! I've come back from the dead' – just when he's sharpening his prized ginsu kitchen knives
- Teaching a fully grown grizzly to dance with you

- Telling your wife you fancy her sister
- Doing four laps of backstroke in a swimming pool filled with acid
- Inhaling near the M25
- Eating a plateful of prime British beef
- Voting the Conservatives back into office

## CARE IN THE COMMUNITY – Some guesses as to how psychiatrists decide that it's safe to release mental patients back into the community

- 'Ip Dip'
- 'One potato, two potato'
- The toss of a coin
- A fast and exciting game of Ker-Plunk!
- They arm-wrestle the psychotic in a best-of-three contest
- They turn their backs and count to 124,455,340,807,890,268,436,000,000
- One of the other psychiatrists dares them to
- The idea for release came to them in a strangely vivid dream
- The Devil told them to do it
- They've just swallowed some prime Valium and everything is OK and tickety-boo . . .
- They got lucky the night before and are feeling good about the world
- They're releasing the psycho in London – and they live in the Outer Hebrides
- They know that they enjoy a total lack of any sort of accountability if anything goes horrifically, bloodily, disastrously wrong

## WILL CARLING – Why it's better to be Will Carling than Albert Einstein

- Albert Einstein never shagged any great birds. Will's had at least two
- Will could duff Albert up if it came to a fight

- No one can understand what Albert was on about; no such problem when Will opens his gob!
- Will didn't help to invent the atomic bomb
- Will has muscles; Albert looked like Albert Steptoe when he got his kit off
- Einstein couldn't score a try against the Scots if his life depended on it
- Will's English; Einstein's a Kraut
- Will's not frightened to shower with other men – there's no record of Einstein ever taking a communal shower with fellow physicists
- When Einstein died, they cut out his brain for medical research. With the greatest respect, Will is hardly likely to suffer the same fate
- Will's nickname is 'Bumface' which is better than being called 'Brainiac' (or 'Mensa Man') as Albert was
- Will has better hair
- Einstein's dead

## CATS – What old ladies think 'Precious' is saying to them

- Hello, I'm so glad you're back from the shops
- I love you, mistress
- Good morning, Mum!
- You're my best friend
- Oh, thank you for my Whiskas Supameat; you're so kind
- I want a cuddle
- Tickle me under the chin
- What's in the shopping basket for me, Mum ? I'm so excited!
- Oh, I do love being with you
- Look. I'm still a kitten at eleven years old!

## CATS – What 'Precious' is *really* saying

- What's that smell? Oh, old mousetrap-feet's home . . .

- Feed me, you loathsome old bitch
- If I was three feet bigger, I'd have you
- Feed me some more, you hag
- Play with me or I'll claw the curtains
- Oy! Cloth-ears! I'm hungry!
- Let me sit on your lap a while. The smell is confusing me and I'm not sure if you're the kitty litter or not
- Feed me, you spiteful old cow!
- God, you're so boring – I think I'll have another nap
- I'll outlive you!
- Arthur's? The couple at 32 give me Felix. That's the last you'll see of me, you old pissbag!

## CENSORSHIP – Terms the Politically Correct brigade prefer to use

- Constructive removal
- Positive exclusion
- Present by absence
- Avoidance confrontation
- Negative positioning
- Accessibly challenged
- Locational otherness
- Differently presented
- Premodified discourse
- Modern college courses
- You're off the faculty!

## CHARITIES – Politically Incorrect ones to give money to

- Fuck the Panda
- Enemies of the Earth
- Greenwar
- The Sod the Children Fund
- Harm a London Child
- The National Con
- Atheist Aid
- Ele-Enemies

- The Anti-Anti-Nazi League
- The RSPCC (The Royal Society for Premeditated Cruelty to Children)
- The RSPB (The Royal Society for the Potting of Birds)
- Anything fronted by a renowned animal killer like Prince Philip

## CHARITIES – Useful excuses when approached by a tin-waving zealot

- *Je ne comprends pas; je suis français*
- I already gave to the lady up the road
- Can you change a £50 note?
- I'm sorry; I was deafened by a V-2 rocket bomb and I can't hear you rattling that tin . . .
- Hey! I gave to Cancer Research last week and you still haven't found a cure . . .
- Charity begins at home – which, coincidentally, is where my wallet is
- I'm Scots
- Charity demeans those it tries to help – so piss off
- I gave last year
- This is all John Major's fault; go wave your tin in front of him
- I only give to charities beginning with the letter X – you have to draw the line somewhere
- I'm sorry; but I don't think that pitiful excuse for a sticker is worth anything
- I haven't given since the ½p was abolished
- You'll only blow the money on poor people or animals or something
- I already support the sick and disabled – I follow West Ham United

## CHARITY SHOPS – Where your money goes

- 8% on Bic razors so the elderly women shop assistants with beards and moustaches can look marginally more like people and not specimens from a geek show

- 12% on de-licing spray to be used on all the donated clothes
- 17% on kitchen towels, cloths and Dettol to clean up after the hordes of incontinent old ladies who spend all day looking for crap
- 10% on air freshener (see above)
- 16% on heavy-duty shelving to withstand the combined weight of smelly *National Geographics*, *Reader's Digests* and Jeffrey Archer paperbacks with bogies sandwiched between every other page
- 20% on clothes rails to be used as shrines to the twin gods of 'bad taste' and 'man-made fibres'
- 15% on the short-term lease from some bastard insurance company landlord who won't rent the site for free
- 2% to the charity involved (of which 'administration' takes 1.75%)

## CHESTY BABES – Things they do that infuriate men

- Wear baggy jumpers
- Always fold their arms across their chests
- Have no interest whatsoever in going trampolining
- Never press themselves up against you on a hot, sweaty, crowded bus (making way for the smelly old pensioner with the open flies to do it instead)
- Claim to have a strong allergy to lycra
- Wear opaque blouses buttoned up to the collar
- Refuse to let you tell their fortune by the lost art of 'Gropology'
- Wear high heels so it's more difficult to look down their dress
- Insist on wearing a bra
- Glare at you when they catch you waggling your tongue at them
- Sunbathe nude in next door's garden
- Sunbathe nude anywhere else

- Never, ever chat you up
- Have big beefy boyfriends

## CHILD LABOUR – Why it's a jolly good idea

- You can pay them less
- If their fingers come off in the machinery, there's less chance of a stoppage
- Trainers are already incredibly expensive. Can you imagine what they'd cost if they weren't produced by child labour? Unthinkable!
- They don't waste time chatting each other up or sneaking out for fags
- If their trade union representative comes to see you, you can put him over your knee and spank him
- It allows adult Pakistanis to sit around all day and smoke dope
- Without child labour, British market traders would have nothing to sell
- You don't need to provide any expensive and wasteful car parking space, as the children all walk the ten miles to the factory
- Without child labour, we wouldn't have vital things like carpets that give you eye strain, bootleg Day-Glo Flintstones T-shirts and bright orange miniature footballs – and civilisation itself might collapse

## CHURCH – Why it's better to play for a pub football team on a Sunday morning than go to church

- You get more satisfaction from a scorching 50-yard volley than you do from a lay reading
- The half-time pep talk is usually more spiritually uplifting than a sermon
- And more comprehensible
- It's easier to remember the words to 'Ere We Go' than it is to 'He Who Would Valiant Be'

- Your subs go on something useful, like new shirts or a match ball rather than the organ restoration fund
- You've got the chance to kick someone you don't like in the shins (this opportunity doesn't often present itself in church)
- You can't shout and swear at your mates in church (well, you can, but it's frowned upon)
- Jesus saves – but then so does your keeper, and you're relying on him to prevent you getting relegated
- You're more likely to find your faith being 2–1 down in a cup match with five minutes left to play

## CIGARETTE ADVERTISING – Claims about smoking that the Advertising Standards Authority should allow

- Smoking makes you a red-hot lover
- It's 100% safe
- It implies you're rich and powerful
- If you don't smoke, you're a loser
- All non-smokers are illegitimate
- 60 a day means you've got an IQ of 185
- If you don't smoke it means you can't afford cigarettes
- If you don't smoke, you're impotent
- Only people with a criminal record don't smoke

## CIGARETTE MACHINES – Politically Incorrect places to install them

- In no-smoking buildings where you're gasping for a fag
- Kindergarten toilets
- Antenatal clinics
- Bronchitis treatment centres
- In the Secretary of State for Health's office
- Right next to the patches on the chemist's counter
- On cancer wards

## CIGARETTES – 10 brands only real rough and tough, don't-give-a-hang he-men would smoke

- Carcinogenic King Sized
- Wheezy Low Tar
- Emphysema Special Tip
- Asthmatic Filter Tip
- Bronchitis Menthol
- Halitosis Extra Length
- Cardio-Vascular Collapse Specials
- Chronic Pneumonia Extra Mild
- Big C 100s
- Mucus Extra Strength

## CIRCUS ANIMALS – 15 more classic acts of yesteryear they should bring back

- Hoppy, kangaroo on a tightrope
- Mahmood the Dromedary – he catches a bullet in his teeth!
- Mr Stripey – the world's only zebra lion tamer!
- Flippy and Floppy, the combustible penguins
- George, the world's only chimpanzee bomb disposal expert
- Jasper and Casper, the tumbling rhinos
- Limpy, donkey on stilts
- Grizzly Dan, the rootin'-tootin', sharpshootin' trick-shot bear
- Mbingo XXXIV, mandrill with a chainsaw
- 'Houdini' Haydn, the underwater escapologist pig
- Luka, the blindfolded flying squirrel
- Harry, the highwire hippo
- Hamish, the marmoset fire-eater on borrowed time
- Mr Bleriot, elephant on a trapeze
- Lumpy and Bumpy, bovine wall of death motorcycle riders extraordinaire

## CJD – Things it helps to explain

- Why there are so many Care in the Community patients
- Why so many Care in the Community patients are let out
- Rave music
- *The Shane Ritchie Experience*
- Noel Gallagher's lyrics
- Welsh
- Why we're still in the EC
- The choice of England managers
- The choice of England players
- The Thatcher years
- Why we believed the government when they said meat was safe
- Why so many of us still believe them today
- Why Dr Who came back

## CJD – Why it can't possibly be the same as BSE

- The initials are different
- They don't start with the same letter at all
- Or end with the same letter
- Or share the same letter in the middle
- If you give A the value of 1 and Z the value of 26, CJD adds up to 17, while BSE adds up to 26. Completely different!
- JDC is an anagram of JCD, not BSE
- If you were doing a crossword and it said 'Brain disease, three letters', and you already had a B in the first square, the answer couldn't possibly be CJD, could it?
- BSE could stand for British Sporting Excellence – CJD couldn't possibly
- If you looked them up in a dictionary, they'd be pages and pages apart!
- CJD is much easier for a ventriloquist's dummy to say than BSE
  BSE infects animals. People aren't animals

- The government says it isn't the same thing
- It would be too terrible to contemplate . . .

## THE CLOSET – 15 places homosexual men are much more likely to come out of

- Freddie Mercury's memorial service
- The men's bogs at Piccadilly Circus
- Fashion college
- The stage door of any theatre
- The staff entrance of any hairdressing salon
- A Derek Jarman all-nighter at the Scala
- Brighton station
- A Hippodrome vogue-athon
- An Erasure gig
- Oxford and Cambridge
- The new MI5 building
- A Bronski Beat reunion gig
- Prince ████████'s private quarters
- The Judy Garland Appreciation Society annual dinner and dance
- A Diana Ross lookalike contest

## COCK-FIGHTING – Some even more Politically Incorrect avian sports

- Linnet-Bashing
- Starling-Thumping
- Crow-Kicking
- Thrush-Biting
- Ostrich-Wrestling
- Thai Raven-Boxing
- Robin Kung Fu
- Chicken Savate
- Tit Judo
- Owl-Pummelling
- Budgie-Jumping-up-and-down-on

## COCKNEYS – Why they should be shot

- They invented the 'knees up'
- They're the only people in the world who think that Pearly Kings and Queens aren't total prats
- They sell you crap goods on their market stalls
- Their rhyming slang is a load of William Pitt
- And a load of Sherman Tank
- Not to mention Joe Loss
- We might get some safe and responsible taxi drivers on the road
- They still think that Moseley was misunderstood
- Their contributions to Western cuisine include such culinary delights as jellied eels, pie and mash, spotted dick, toad in the hole and salmonella

## COCOONING – Why it's better to stay indoors than go out

- Immediate members of your family are less likely to mug you
- Your partner is probably not high on crack and desperate for their next fix
- You are unlikely to encounter a road-rager in your bathroom
- Care in the Community patients are not rehoused in your dining room – yet
- The Yorkshire Ripper never attacked anyone in a conservatory
- If you're going to try hitch-hiking, it's far safer to do it in the hallway
- Few, if any, of us have ever been pickpocketed on our way to the pantry
- Flashers are more likely to be found in the park after dark rather than your living room during Noel's *Telly Addicts*
- Carjackers will have trouble getting you in the kitchenette
- If you go out, the burglars will get in . . .

## COLONIAL GUILT – Why guilt is the last thing you should feel

- They wanted independence. It's not our fault they've had a bloody civil war for the past fifty years
- Syphilis would have reached them eventually, anyway
- All right, so we took their mineral wealth, but we gave them cricket
- Just because we lived there doesn't mean they should live here
- If we hadn't invaded India, Gandhi wouldn't have had a chance to shine and we'd be down one brilliant movie
- Down two, if you count *Zulu*, which is also great
- Without those proud men who built the Empire, you wouldn't be able to get a decent biriani after chucking-out time anywhere
- If we hadn't invaded them, the French Empire would have got them and they'd all be sitting around Bongo-Bongo Land smoking Gauloise and eating quiche. No, actually, they'd probably all be in Paris, driving taxis
- If we hadn't invaded them, the German Empire would have got them and they'd all be speaking Kraut and eating cabbage. No, actually, they'd probably all be dead

## THE COMMONWEALTH – How we could improve it

- Throw out all the crappy Third World countries
- Invite rich countries like America and Japan to join
- Get rid of all that ethnic crap in the Commonwealth Institute and turn it into an indoor go-kart arena
- Don't allow any country in that can play half-decent cricket
- Throw out the Queen and make Pamela Anderson titular head

- Scrap Commonwealth summits and replace them with Commonwealth paint ball tournaments (Third World countries never have anything to say worth listening to – but it's very satisfying to shoot a fat be-medalled despot in the head with a paint pellet)
- Stop calling it something dull and liberal and wishy-washy like 'The Commonwealth' and call it something more exciting like 'Earth Strikeforce Alliance'
- Or 'The British Empire'

## COMPASSION FATIGUE – Why you're probably feeling it

- You bought two Jeffrey Archer paperbacks in Oxfam last week and there's still famine in Africa
- You put a fiver on the Lottery every week and no one's discovered a cure for cancer yet (plus, you haven't even won £10 yet)
- Last year they said, with your help, they could beat cystic fibrosis. They lied . . .
- They tell you that £1 can buy a blanket. What use is that?
- They tell you £1 could buy a blanket. And you know it's a lie because you can't buy a blanket at that price anywhere (not even off the market)
- You want to help. They say 'Give a man a fish and he eats for a day. Teach him to fish and he eats for life.' The only thing is, you don't know the first thing about angling – and you think it's cruel, anyway
- He is your brother – and he *is* bloody heavy

## CONDOMS – Why they're a stupid idea

- You get all embarrassed asking for them in chemists'
- You have to make excuses while you're desperately trying to put them on 'Mr Wobbly'

- They fall out of your wallet or pocket at the most inopportune moments
- You can never remember which drawer you've hidden them in
- Your mum usually finds them in your room
- They're only 98% safe
- They're expensive
- They're usually too big
- That horrible spermicide stuff gets in your hair, your fingers, your mouth and everywhere
- The reason they come in packets of three is that you usually ruin at least two of them trying to put them on
- They can unroll on their own and ping off the end of your nob
- Safe sex is for cowards

## CONFESSIONAL BOOTHS – What they're good for

- Developing film
- A quickie
- Playing 'Murder in the Dark'
- Punch and Judy shows
- Going 'dung-de-dung, dung-de-dung' and pretending you're in the Tardis
- A magician's prop cabinet
- Starting your own Photo-Me booth
- A changing cubicle
- Having a crafty wank between services

## THE CONSERVATIVE PARTY – 7 brand-new ways it can increase its funding

- Sell knighthoods (oh no, it's already doing that)
- Accept contributions from crooks (and that . . .)
- Take generous donations from suspected war criminals to help curry favour (and that too. Have they thought of everything?)

- Privatise more companies, so there are more private companies to make donations to Conservative Party coffers. (They have . . .?)
- Er . . .
- Um . . .
- Well . . .

## CONTRACEPTION – Why doctors should give the pill to fourteen-year-old girls

- So fourteen-year-old boys don't suddenly find they've become fathers
- So 34-year-old teachers don't suddenly find they've become fathers – and unemployed
- It's better than giving it to twelve-year-old girls
- It means that their boyfriends don't have to waste their pocket money on condoms
- It gives doctors the chance to get a fourteen-year-old girl alone in the surgery (a chance not to be sneezed at)
- It prevents them getting pregnant and missing important parts of the National Curriculum like GCSE biology
- It prevents them getting pregnant and bumming a free flat off the council which can instead go to someone more needy (like a pregnant thirteen-year-old girl)

## CONVICTS – Why we should still be deporting them to Australia

- It was their kind who made Australia what it is today
- It can only improve the Australian breeding stock
- They'd never notice an extra ten thousand thieving morons
- Or an extra million for that matter
- They send all their scum over here

- The violent criminals might come in useful for the national pastime of 'picking on the Abos'
- The really violent criminals might come in useful for the other national pastime of rugby
- It's cheaper to give them a one-way ticket on Qantas than banging them up in jail for even one day
- Australia is worse than any jail and fear of being sent there would deter even the most hardened of criminals

## CORPORAL PUNISHMENT – Why it should be reintroduced

- Judges might actually start to punish young offenders – as long as they could do it personally – and kiss it all better afterwards
- It's hard to joyride when your arse is so sore you can't sit down
- The British slipper industry would come out of the doldrums
- We could film the punishment and sell it as a pervie movie to the Germans
- You try climbing up someone's drainpipe when you've just had six strokes of the cane on both palms
- It couldn't hurt
- (But we sincerely hope that it does)

## A COUNCIL FLAT – The 12 most likely people to receive one instantly

- Algerian Uniped Lesbian Mime Troupe Political Agitators
- Lebanese One-Parent Travellers
- Bisexual Gypsies with learning difficulties
- Attention Deficit Syndrome Black Dwarves with rabies
- Masectomised Bangladeshis with homosexual dogs

- Battered Somali men who think they're women trapped in men's bodies
- Marxist Feminist Prostitutes with exceptionally hairy armpits
- Homeless repeat offenders with influential parole officers
- Special-needs alcoholic cross-dressers with learning difficulties
- Literacy-Challenged Homeless Inuits with no refugee status
- Sex offenders on their eighth 'last chance'
- Irish terrorists

## A COUNCIL FLAT – The people likely never to receive one

- Ordinary people
- People who deserve it
- People who genuinely need it

## COUNTRIES – 13 that sound like awful diseases

- Malawi (uncontrollable vomiting spasms)
- Tonga (a polyp in the colon)
- Anguilla (painful inflammation of the joints)
- Hong Kong (a painful discharge from the penis)
- Botswana (unrelenting diarrhoea)
- Belize (a nasty skin condition)
- Fiji (something you catch if you don't use a condom)
- Haiti (exceptional itching of the scrotal sac)
- Maldives (a form of pubic lice infestation)
- Monaco (only having one descended testicle)
- Peru (blood in your stools)
- Syria (incontinence)
- Zimbabwe (large boils covering over 75% of the surface of your skin)

## THE COUNTRY OF THE BLIND – 3 people other than the 'One-Eyed Man' who are king

- Anyone that can discern vague shapes
- Anyone that's just colour blind
- The Two-Eyed Man

## COWS – Other uses for them now that we can't eat them any more

- Large but effective draught excluders
- Slow but determined lawn mowers
- Horses for people who are frightened of horses
- Woolworths sales staff
- Cows bedecked with tinsel and covered in fake snow make super Christmas ornaments
- Bungee-jump rope testers
- Pets for people with ostentatiously large rooms
- An ultra-realistic alternative to the traditional pantomime cow
- A welcome sight for homesick Hindus
- Providing a slow but entertaining alternative to greyhound racing
- Crash test dummies
- As an integral part of Project 'Hey Diddle Diddle', Britain's attempt to put a cow into space
- Ballast for oil tankers
- Suspend them from a chain and use them as some new sort of wrecking ball
- Target practice for a NATO exercise on Dartmoor
- Paint them silver and sell them to a woman giant as lucky charms for her bracelet
- Take two of them to a nearby river and play a slight variation of the game Pooh Sticks
- Kill them, chop them up and use them for animal feed

## CRICKET – How we can make this British sporting tradition much more exciting

- Play soccer but call it cricket
- Allow players running between wickets to be shot at by outfielders
- Bowlers should be allowed to aim at the face so batsman can be carried off, face before wicket
- Naked women should run across the turf every seven minutes throughout the event
- Batsmen should be forced to perform fellatio on a 70-year-old vagrant every time they play a safe shot
- Sensible white slacks should be replaced with black leather bondage thongs
- Wicket-keepers should be allowed to use kung fu on batsmen
- Batsmen should be allowed to use bats on wicket-keepers
- Murray Walker should be called in to spice up the commentary
- The player at silly mid-on should be called 'The Axeman' – with good reason
- The slip should be mined
- Nobody British should be allowed to play it

## CRYSTALS – Their real powers, revealed

- Amethyst – May hurt if you fall on it in your pocket!
- Rose Quartz – May give you stomach ache if you swallow it!
- Tourmaline – Prevents hearing if you jam it in your ear!
- Aquamarine – Can easily be lost at the bottom of your handbag or purse!
- Carnelian – Stays in your hand if you hold on to it!
- Jade – Looks astonishingly like a crystal!
- Ruby – Will never become a piece of cheese!
- Coral – Will not do anything if you put it in your car!

## DALEKS– Why the next Prime Minister should be a Dalek

- It'd scare the shit out of the Queen at the state opening of Parliament
- Instead of negotiating with the trade unions, it would simply tell them, 'You-Will-Obey! Obey-the-will-of-the-Daleks-or-die!'
- Jeremy smug-boy Paxman wouldn't last two seconds (unless he was able to run up some stairs)
- It would be the first time in history you could merchandise a PM
- How long have we waited for a British Prime Minister to stand up in Maastricht and say, 'We-Are-The-Master-Race! We-Are-Supreme!'
- Instead of exchanging witticisms at Prime Minister's Question Time, it could just yell 'Exterminate! Exterminate!' and spray the opposite benches with laser fire – and not before time, too
- Inside each Dalek is a slimy blob of corrupted tissue – this could be the big break John Redwood has been looking for!
- Or Edwina Currie, thus guaranteeing another Tory-dominated Parliament

- The Chancellor of the Exchequer wouldn't be able to pull any more fast ones, because the Dalek Prime Minister's robot brain would check the calculations and then start yelling 'Does-not-compute – does-not-compute!', spinning around in panic and blasting everything with its laser arm
- There would be no more unemployment, as the out-of-work would become slaves in the Dalek mines
- Have you noticed how much Davros looks like ex-Prime Minister Margaret Thatcher – and what a great PM she was!
- It would still be more human than any other Prime Minister we've had

## DATING – Why it's better to go on a hot date with Pamela Anderson, rather than Sooty

- Friends and workmates will not be nearly so impressed if you tell them you've scored a date with Sooty
- Sooty is notoriously flat-chested
- Sooty can't play footsy under the table with you, because he hasn't got any feet
- If Sooty tried to run along the beach in *Baywatch* like a sensuous sea goddess he wouldn't get very far
- Sooty is liable to spend all evening either showing you tricks with his magic wand or spraying you with a little water pistol
- Pamela is a better conversationalist – marginally
- Sooty is only little and has to be home by ten o'clock
- There's no chance of a slow smoochy dance with Sooty because he'd only reach halfway up your shin
- Everyone will know what happened on your date, because Sooty will whisper it all in Mr Corbett's ear
- Sooty isn't real

- Neither is Pamela Anderson – but who cares?

## DATING – Why it's better to go out with Sooty rather than Janet Street Porter

- Sooty can't talk

## DEF LEPPARD – Why they're better than Beethoven

- None of Beethoven's recordings ever went triple platinum
- Def Leppard's Rick Allen lost his arm in a car crash whereas Beethoven only went deaf (the big wuss)
- Def Leppard have a tasty logo but Beethoven only used his boring old signature
- Beethoven began as a court musician aged nineteen, whereas Joe Elliot formed Def Leppard when he was eighteen
- Beethoven sold less copies of his nine symphonies, seven concertos and 32 piano sonatas than Def Leppard's five albums; proof of quality over quantity
- No matter how hard you try, you can't headbang (or slamdance) to the Pastoral Symphony
- Def Leppard have clawed their way to the top with talent, guts and determination; Beethoven was sponsored by a rich patron, the Archduke Randolph
- Beethoven never embarked on a sell-out tour of the US (although he did play to the Viennese aristocracy)
- All of Def Leppard (except Phil Collen) have had longer hair than Beethoven
- Beethoven left an unfinished symphony whereas Def Leppard have had the common courtesy to complete all their contractual obligations

## DEMOCRACY – Why it's rubbish

- It puts politicians into power
- It puts the Tories into power

- You know that the Tories and the Labour Party could run mentally retarded apes for Parliament and they'd still win
- You know that they do
- What's the alternative? The Liberals? Do me a favour . . .
- People who read the *Sun* can vote
- Banana republics have all the jazziest national anthems
- No party has EVER won by one vote – proving that your vote doesn't count for very much
- No matter who you vote for, they always lose
- No matter who you vote for, they let you down the moment they're elected
- No matter how many times you vote, things never change

## DEMONSTRATION MARCHES – Why they should be banned

- They slow the traffic down to a halt, infuriating drivers and making them antagonistic towards the cause
- Why bother to march when it's far easier just to post a petition to Downing Street?
- Or write to the *Daily Mail* letters page?
- Most of the marchers are scruffy and are bad PR for the cause
- It embarrasses the police escort since people might think they're there because they support the cause
- The banners and placards are full of weary clichés and platitudes
- And all have *Socialist Worker* printed on them
- Gay rights activists marching through the streets, tonguing each other, is very off-putting when you're just trying to do your Saturday shop
- Unless they end in violence, the marchers won't appear on the news and get the publicity they set out to achieve

- No one marches for important issues that affect you like 'Chesty Babes on the National Health!' or '100% Pay Increase for Everyone, Now!'
- The government just ignores the whole thing anyway

## DIESEL CARS – Why they're crap

- You have to wait for the little light to go off before starting the engine, adding an eternity to your journey
- You might be tempted to speed just to make up this lost time
- Myopic people try and flag you down because they think you're a taxi
- Because you fill them up with fuel less frequently it takes you twice as long to save up Shell vouchers – and then they've run out of Bon Jovi albums and you have to settle for four tumblers, one of which is broken
- It doesn't do much for your street cred filling your car up with the same fuel a tractor uses
- They're more expensive than petrol equivalents yet they don't even come with spark plugs!
- You only save 1p per gallon when you fill up
- Most garages only have one diesel pump and you usually have to wait your turn behind a Belgian juggernaut filling each of its three 80-gallon tanks
- If they're so good then why doesn't Ferrari make them?

## DIPLOMATIC IMMUNITY – What it really allows you to do

- Get pissed and drive the wrong way up one-way streets until you kill a family of four in a fireball
- Hump a young British boy with your three cousins
- Cruise for tarts who would be stoned to death in your shit-wipe home country

- Bring half a hundredweight of uncut smack, 50 lb of Semtex and four snuff movies into the country inside a bulging diplomatic bag
- Shoot WPCs
- Try and beat the 1993 Nigerian record for 'Most parking fines unpaid in a sovereign state'
- Try and beat the 1994 United Arab Emirates' record for 'Most boy scouts deflowered by a high-ranking attaché in 24 hours'
- Try and beat the 1992 Yemeni record for 'Most expensive item stolen from Marks and Spencer's at Marble Arch'
- Try and beat the 1991 Iraqi record for 'Most public place to openly masturbate'
- Carry a gun big enough to shoot down an airliner
- Flick V-signs at the custody officer
- Anything else you damn well like

## DISCRIMINATION – Why it's good

- Without discrimination there'd be no one to live in the ghettos
- It makes choosing a new employee very easy and cost-efficient
- Without it there'd be no one to do the jobs that no one else wants
- It gives you someone to blame for all your problems
- Without discrimination there wouldn't be such a thing as 'privilege'
- It gives minorities the impetus they need to try that much harder

## DISCRIMINATION – Why it's wrong to discriminate against white males

- That's not the way it's supposed to be done

## DISRUPTIVE PUPILS – Why they *should* be allowed into schools

- While they're in school, they're not in your car
- Or your house
- Judges won't send them to jail, where they belong
- Let those smug liberal bastard teachers experience some real life for once
- You can withdraw your child, secure in the knowledge that the troublemaker is confined
- If schools expelled all mindlessly violent pupils, half the comprehensives in London could be relocated in a bus shelter
- The same bus shelter

## THE DODO – Why we should be glad it's extinct

- It was a crap bird
- It was fucking ugly
- It tasted like Evo-Stick
- It had a stupid name and you'd be embarrassed to admit you had one as a pet
- If it wasn't extinct, the phrase 'dead as a dodo' would, frankly, be meaningless and the English language would be impoverished because of it
- Dodo feathers were full of parasites and would never have been suited to quilts and eiderdowns
- If it wasn't, all kinds of do-gooders would be after our cash to help prevent its extinction
- It serves as a warning to other birds that dare to get in the way of man's progress

## DOG-FIGHTING – Why and how it should become a national sport

- It's as humane as boxing
- It could be just like boxing; a league for flyweights (Yorkshire terriers, poodles, Chihuahuas), middleweights (collies, retrievers, Labradors, larger

spaniels and setters) and heavyweights (Alsatians, Dobermanns and Rottweilers)

- Instead of 'Eye of the Tiger', fighting dogs could make a grand entrance to a rousing version of 'How Much Is That Doggy in the Window?'
- Fighting dogs could have dramatic nicknames like 'Iron Mike Fido', 'Boom-Boom Basset Hound' and 'Smoking Joe Beagle'
- Lassie could provide a ringside commentary
- Star fighting dogs could appear in panto – as long as the theatre was heavily insured
- It would always be a fair fight; it's hard to train a dog to 'take a dive in the fifth' (they can't count, as much as anything else . . .)
- As usual, everyone would be cheering for the underdog
- One throat wound or one punctured intestine could decide the winner

## DOLE – Industries that would benefit if we slashed it

- Cardboard box manufacturers
- Makers of filthy tattered old blankets
- British Gas
- The manufacturers of Paracetamol
- Places charging admission to high buildings or bridges
- Sales of razor blades and Super Matey bubble bath
- Platform tickets on mainline stations with lots of non-stop expresses thundering through at 100 mph
- Sales of petrol and Swan Vestas
- Shotguns

## DOLE – Industries that would suffer if we slashed it

- Breweries
- Tobacco companies
- The bookies
- Bingo halls
- Sky TV subscription channels

- CD sales
- Illegal pit bull breeding
- The Spanish tourist industry
- Camelot

## DOLE OFFICE – 11 types you always see there

- Someone you just know has a machete under that bomber jacket
- The athletic sort who tries to climb over the protective barrier to get at the staff
- Someone who speaks no language known to man – and has a scrappy handwritten note in the same language which he's trying to get the person behind the counter to read
- Some bloke in a donkey jacket who takes you aside and says, 'Psst! John, you interested in the dogfightin', then?'
- A blonde with four-inch black roots dragging two ginger-haired half-caste children backwards by their wrists
- Minicab drivers between shifts
- Anyone else between shifts
- Men over 40 with not a hope in hell of ever, ever, ever finding another job
- Extras from *Quest for Fire*
- Care in the Community types talking to their packet of crisps
- Writers trying to live off publishers' royalties

## DOLE OFFICE – Good things to do there

- Pull up outside in your new BMW then set fire to it and casually walk away
- Pop your head round the door and say loudly, 'So this is where all the layabouts hang out'
- Go inside and count everyone very loudly. When someone asks what you're doing say that you're adding up the number of 'losers' in the borough

- Go inside, count everyone very loudly, then divide the total by two. When someone asks what you're doing say that you're compiling the official government unemployment statistics
- Demoralise everyone even more by telling them that you've been out of work for seven years, during which time you've applied for 4,472 jobs – and got two interviews
- Sign on using a Mont Blanc pen just to make everyone jealous
- Start a mass panic by shouting at the clerk, 'Do you mean to say that under new EU law our benefit has been slashed to two quid a week!'
- Taunt everyone by flaunting your latest payslip

## DONOR CARDS – Why you should refuse to carry one

- Your vital organs will be creamed off to some rich Arab in a private practice in Harley Street, not some needy kid
- If God has special plans for someone, He might decide to bump you off so that they can get your liver
- Anyone arriving in A & E with a donor card is 'fair game' – whether you're really dead or not
- The doctors can't be arsed to put you back together again after they've cannibalised you and your relatives end up with a sack of skin, bones and offal
- Your relatives should be paid for your organs, since the doctors will be making a mint
- Do you really want part of you to go on living inside some rich bastard businessman who's ruthless enough to jump the queue to get your organs?
- You might mistake it for your credit card and look stupid in front of all the shoppers when the supermarket refuses to accept it

- You don't know whose body you might end up in. Your kidney could be forced to live out its life as a woman . . .
- You don't get *Profiles* points every time you use it
- The transplant team won't thank you if they have to get out of bed and dash to a hospital at 4 a.m. on a Sunday morning
- If there's reincarnation you'll come back without kidneys and instantly die (*ad infinitum*)
- We can get all the kidneys we need just by buying them from impoverished people in the Third World

## DOUBLE GLAZING SALESMEN – Why they should pick on the elderly

- If they didn't pick on them, fitted kitchen salesmen would
- They're the only people gullible enough to fall for their sales pitch
- How else are they going to earn such easy commissions?
- It eases them into the job of high-pressure selling, gently
- While they're in the house they can case it for valuables
- Writing to *That's Life* to complain gives the elderly something to do
- While they're out selling to the elderly they're not pestering you
- The elderly today have the most disposable income and are one of the few groups in society able to afford £2,500 for a few bits of glass and some plastic frames
- It enables salesmen to exploit the old 'Double glazing makes it harder for burglars to break in . . . Hey! That sounded like someone creeping about!' routine

## DRACULA – Why he's Politically Incorrect

- He's white
- He's male
- He's a count
- He lives in a castle
- He discriminates against men in his blood lust
- He orders wolves about
- He turns into a polluting fog
- He has lots of 'brides'
- He tells gypsies what to do

## DRIVERS – Why men are better drivers than women

- They get there faster than women (this is true of many things men do)
- They know more rude words to use on each other
- They're faster on the horn
- They *know* when they can beat the lights
- They can take corners at far greater speeds
- They can change lanes in the tightest of spaces
- They *know* they can drive OK, even when they're drunk
- A man can beat any woman in accelerating away at the lights, regardless of his car

## DRUG DEALERS – Why they're a boon to society

- Without them, sales of H-reg BMWs with 200-watt sound systems would plummet
- They spend so much time on mobile phones, they almost subsidise the cost of calls for the rest of us
- They prove to kids from housing estates that free enterprise is the route to success
- Who else can afford £165 trainers?
- Or £2,000 worth of Rolex?
- Without them, *The Bill* would be stretched for plots and a wonderful soap would grind to a halt

- They keep the Customs and Excise officers busy, preventing them from springing any more surprise VAT inspections on us
- It's reassuring for parents to know that the young men who hang around inner-city school gates aren't child molesters
- They keep the gold jewellery market buoyant
- They generate employment in deprived areas for all sorts of occupations, e.g. drivers, look-outs, bodyguards, couriers and hit-men

## GERALD DURRELL – Some Politically Incorrect books he should have written

- The Homeless and Other Parasites
- The Old and Other Millstones
- Conscientious Objectors and Other Cowards
- Asylum Seekers and Other Burdens on the State
- The Third World and Other Shitholes
- Buskers and Other Dossers
- Liberals and Other Tossers
- The Unemployed and Other Scroungers
- Women and Other People Just Gagging for It
- Authors and Other People Abusing Freedom of Speech

## DWARF THROWING – Other events that give the seriously vertically challenged a chance of participating in sport

- Runt Basketball
- Squirt Jumping
- Titch Boxing
- The Shortarse Javelin
- Pygmy Rugby
- Pee-Wee Ping-Pong
- Half-Pint Hurdling
- Tossing the Shrimp
- Crotchsniffer Cricket

- You Down There Lacrosse
- Squat Ice Hockey
- Smallfry Pole Vaulting
- Clay Pigeon Dinky Shooting

**DYSLEXICS – And now some special jokes for dyslexia sufferers, just so they don't feel left out of the reading experience**

- Sghrtip optyil sdcty! (yitkl gashehtytiy!!!!)
- Sjkuy – syrbk – deyjk!
- Dks suorykuyhjhf iefgmktgaot, sfjtykig, ohsthcjnkl!
- Aghehi dhuyuknj opdggnyhthr afojyhk?
- Lsfhkkj ufggnj, dguilghlawxxe, zzzxsxs
- zzzxsxs, zzzxsxs dfg zzzxsxs!

## ECO-WARRIORS – Why they're a crap fighting force

- Tree-hugging is not a recognised offensive manoeuvre used by any of the world's élite fighting forces
- Torpedoes or a deck-mounted 105mm cannon are more likely to stop a Japanese whaling ship than an inflatable dinghy, a clenched fist and an old Joan Baez cassette
- Painting the 'Peace' symbol on your face will not strike fear into the hearts of enemies; an ear necklace will
- Chaining yourself to a bulldozer is not as effective as sticking magnetic mines to its fuel tank
- You present less of a target to the enemy if you're in a trench or a bunker rather than the treetops or manacled to a chain-link fence
- The enemy is more wary of an opponent who knows how to kill a man with his bare hands than one who knows how to climb a tree
- Shooting Canadian seal cullers with a video camera won't stop them. Shooting them with an AK-47 will

## ECSTASY – Why it's far better than aspirin

- It's far cooler to take Ecstasy at a rave than aspirin
- Aspirin could soon lead you on to other drugs – like Paracetamol
- You can't make big money pushing aspirin (and you'd get laughed at)
- Aspirin bottles are left in a bathroom cabinet, putting temptation within reach of children. Ecstasy tablets are always well hidden so there's no danger of this
- If you asked rave-goers 'Are you sorted for A?' they'd think you were on drugs
- You can break your fingernails trying to remove the safety cap on a bottle of aspirin
- With Junior Disprin, aspirin manufacturers openly and unashamedly target young users
- Ecstasy tablets come in nice colours like brown, pink or yellow; aspirins are just boring white
- Girls will do it with you to score half a tab of E; any girl who does it with you for an aspirin is probably mental
- Any drug that you can buy over the counter at Boots doesn't have a lot of street cred
- Jungle sounds great if you've taken Ecstasy. Aspirin only stops the headache it gives you if you're straight
- Taking too much aspirin will result in severe stomach cramps; you don't have this problem with taking too much Ecstasy since you'll be dead

## EIGHTEEN – Why it's better to shag two 18-year-old girls than cure poverty and disease

- It just is
- Your friends will be much more impressed by a Casanova than a do-gooder
- Which letter is *Penthouse* most likely to publish – the one about you shagging two eighteen-year-olds

or the one where you bring new wealth to the Third World?

- Helping others may be good for the soul – but there's no proof you have a soul; whereas you can be absolutely certain you have a libido (unless you're Matthew Kelly)
- A blow-job is better than a Nobel Prize, any old day of the week
- It's considerably easier to cure poverty and disease than it is to persuade two eighteen-year-olds to go to bed with you

## EL PRESIDENTE – Why it's good to be a fascist dictator

- If your neighbour doesn't return your hedge strimmer, you can make him 'disappear'
- You can wear kinky jodhpurs and leather boots and no one will laugh
- If the paper boy is late, you can turn him over to the death squads
- You can wear sunglasses indoors and not feel like a prat
- You can borrow your secret police's torture equipment for kinky sex romps
- You can borrow your secret police for kinky sex romps
- If the milkman forgets to leave your yoghurt, you can satisfy yourself with the knowledge that his days as a 'man' are numbered
- Waiters will never seat you next to the toilets for fear of being found with their severed penis stuffed into an empty eye socket
- GCSEs are less important than animal cunning
- Two imperial guardsmen standing outside your maisonette look more impressive than garden gnomes
- It's better to be known as 'El Diablo' than 'that fat git at number 19'

- The CIA will give you lots of money
- And guns

## THE ELDERLY – Why it's unwise for companies to employ anyone over 60

- They spend ten minutes out of every hour in the bogs, changing their incontinence pants
- Their hearing aids might cause electrical interference with the sophisticated fire alarm system
- They'll drive the other staff mental by continuously saying, 'In my day . . .' (followed by some crap)
- It'll cost £288,000 just to install a Stannah stair lift in a typical sixteen-storey office block
- Their Zimmer frames will block the doorway in the event of a fire
- They'll embarrass an important client by taking their false teeth out in the middle of a meeting
- . . . Or being mega-flatulent
- A B-reg Austin Maxi or Morris Marina in the office car park doesn't leave the best impression
- They'll spend all day trying to work out what a computer does
- Or is
- They'll be forever looking out of the window and daydreaming about getting their pension
- Or Rita Hayworth
- One phone call too many on a busy day and they go into cardiac arrest
- You can't get any work done because you're too busy giggling at their obvious wigs
- They're always going to the hospital for a bypass or whatever
- They call secretaries 'dolly birds'
- They wear brown BHS suits
- They spend hours telling you about how they coped before the fax machine was invented

- Or the typewriter
- Or the wheel
- Or any form of spoken communication
- They know ten times as much as you ever will and constantly make you look bad

## ELECTRIC-SHOCK BATONS – Why they're a good thing

- They're much more humane than 'Chainsaw Batons' or 'Batons that Fire Poison Darts that Embed Themselves in Your Bollocks'
- Gas-powered ones would pollute the atmosphere
- Nuclear-powered ones would have to be stored in ten-feet-thick lead containers between beatings
- Coal-fired ones would be impractical, taking close on 48 hours to generate a paltry twelve volts
- Clockwork ones could wind down just as the victim is about to spill everything . . .
- Wave-powered batons are of limited use in desert states
- Elaborate shock batons, where the electricity is generated by a second man pedalling a bicycle, reduce the whole interrogation to the level of farce
- They give documentary film-makers an excuse to visit Saudi Arabia and South America
- They give documentary film-makers' PAs a chance to visit these countries as well and get a nice tan
- They keep Amnesty International on their toes
- Without them, the editorial and advertising staff working for *Which Electric-Shock Baton?* would all be out of a job
- They give men a chance to understand the discomfort women have to endure during electrolysis
- They can help cure hiccups
- On a low setting, they can provide many a night's pleasure for the lonely Arab

- They're a great impulse buy – which is why you always find them by the check-out at Weapons R Us

## ENDANGERED SPECIES – What burger chains should consider selling (here's some food for thought . . .)

- Rhino Nuggets
- Whalemeat 2,200-pounder with cheese
- Spicy Golden Eagle
- Big Panda
- Lemur Muffin
- McMarmoset
- Gorilla in a Bap
- Bison on a Stick
- Fillet-o-Giant Anteater
- Flame-Grilled Sumatran Tiger
- Condor Drumsticks
- Bucket of Orang-Utan
- Nile Crocodile Dippers
- Elephant Whopper
- Koala Double Cheeseburgers

## ENGLISH – Why it's the best language in the whole world

- The Eskimos might have sixteen words for 'snow' but we've got eighteen words for 'vagina'
- And 37 for 'penis' (OK, so we're lighter on words for testicles, but we've still got loads more than the blubberheads)
- It's so versatile that you can make some words dirty just by changing one single letter, e.g. 'tanker', 'runt', 'ship' – even 'motherducker'
- *Double entendres* make even the most innocent sentence sound dirty. E.g. a farmer might be training his hens to ride miniature motorcycles when one of the males goes missing while it's raining. In a case like this you might say, 'Have you

73

seen my big cock? You know, the one with the glistening purple helmet?'
- It provides loads of dirty words that rhyme – essential when writing rude poetry or songs, e.g. suck/fuck, clit/tit – even masturbation/ejaculation. It's as if whoever invented the English language wanted us to write rude rhymes!

## EPILEPTICS – How they could be put to good use

- Grape-crushing in wine-producing countries
- As a valuable form of kinetic energy we could harness as a power source
- They could be employed as government advisers and help to thrash things out
- In any future remake of *The Exorcist*
- As a handy way of turning your bath into a washing machine
- As whirling dervishes
- As a way of turning ordinary bathtubs into luxury jacuzzis
- Starting a new craze on the nation's dance floors
- To get every sodding Nintendo and Sega Megadrive banned

## ESPERANTO – What we'd miss if we all spoke this universal language

- The ability to smile at a foreigner while saying, 'You're an ugly Kraut git and your wife has a face like my cat's botty' without them having any idea of what you're going on about
- The ability to modify language so you could call anyone who's fat and whiffy 'a person of size and alternative body fragrance'
- Julian Clary, Dale Winton and John Inman (how on earth would they make a living without the *double entendre*? Er, that was a rhetorical question. You don't have to answer that, even if you do have ideas . . .)

## ESSEX – Things it's pointless to try and establish there

- Arts centres
- A branch of MENSA
- Businesses requiring skilled labour
- A chain of fine art shops
- A classical record shop
- Deportment schools
- Schools teaching proper speech
- Respect for law and order
- Higher education
- Lower education
- Pretty much anything except fun pubs, really

## ETHIOPIANS – Why they're lucky

- They've got a head start if they want to be supermodels – they've got figures to die for . . .
- They don't indulge themselves with life-threatening diseases like anorexia and bulimia
- They don't have to pay for their food
- They get on telly and can wave to their mums (if their mums are still alive)
- They've probably met Tony Robinson
- They don't have to spend all day slaving out in the fields – because nothing grows there
- They can sit around all day and do nothing
- If they have a penchant for pet flies, they're well sorted!
- Top comics go over and make them laugh – for free!
- Their government is free to spend all its money on weapons
- They don't live in Britain

## ETHNIC CUSTOMS AND TRADITIONS – Why we should have nothing but contempt for them

- They're as crappy, boring, barbaric and ridiculous as our own

- They usually involve disembowelling, beheading or buggering some animal
- They're also usually blatantly and brutally sexist, but we mustn't allow that to sway our contempt for them
- Germans have a well-established tradition of genocide – shall we respect that?
- Black kids in huge baggy trousers and back-to-front baseball caps are not making an ethnic statement – they're just dressed like dildoes
- Liberal wishy-washy teachers think that it's valuable that your kid should spend his or her school time doing paintings and decorations for the ancient Aztec feast of Txrzjhbkzydx, instead of maths and English
- Why should we let people shag chickens at the summer equinox just because they've been doing it for years and years?
- In India, it was once customary for a wife to throw herself on her husband's funeral pyre. How do you fancy that one, ladies?
- And now on to the subject of female circumcision . . .
  *(Not in this book – Ed)*


## ETHNIC FOOD – Why it's crap

- It's far easier to say 'Double egg and chips, please, luv' than 'Rogan josh with aloo gobi and bhindi bhaji, pronto, Gunga Din!'
- If you've got the munchies at midnight it's far easier to make yourself a cheese and pickle sarnie than to rustle up Kung Po chicken in black bean sauce with green peppers
- You can't accidentally put your hand on a hot-plate and scald yourself when you're making tripe and onions

- Most of it was originally invented by people so hungry they had to eat the most disgusting things known to man
- No lobsters were ever boiled alive in the preparation of Yorkshire pud
- Moussaka has never come first in a black pudding contest
- The average Indian takeaway takes fifteen minutes; you can pick up cod, chips and a saveloy instantly
- If God had wanted us to eat raw fish, he wouldn't have invented deep fat fryers
- If God had wanted us to eat Indian, he'd have given us asbestos rectums

## ETHNIC IDENTITY – Some typical times when you might want to claim yours

- When you want a council flat
- When you want to get out of boring RE lessons
- When you want a lottery grant of £100,000 to paint with your feet
- When you don't fancy what's on the airline menu
- When you meet a simply scrummy goat and there's no one about . . .
- When you want a job with Lambeth Council
- When you're in a Los Angeles courtroom and it's patently obvious you murdered your wife

## EUROPE – What are our taxes really paying for?

- 400,000 French cows that don't really exist
- Several hundred theoretical Italian vineyards
- Two nights a week with two very luscious Brussels call-girls
- The Sardinian Mafia's drug stake money
- A court that's biased against us
- 400,000 pretend chickens in Ireland
- Jacques Santer's penis-enlarging treatments
- 600,000 virtual Belgian sheep
- Big subsidies to bone-idle French peasants

- Conjectural German banana plantations
- Hypothetical cornfields in the Dordogne
- Even bigger subsidies to Spanish fishermen to come over here and steal our fish because their home waters are too filthy to sustain life

## THE EUROPEAN COURT OF HUMAN RIGHTS – 12 things it takes into consideration when reaching its verdicts

- Will this piss off Britain?
- Will this outrage decent ordinary people?
- Will this fly in the face of common sense?
- Will this give comfort and succour to terrorists and murderers?
- Is this the judgement of complete arseholes with no grip on reality?
- Will this make the Germans happy?
- Will this make the IRA ecstatic?
- Will this make the evening news?
- Will this sound like it came out of our arses?
- Have we failed to misunderstand enough?
- Is this the wrong verdict?
- Will our supreme master, Satan, be pleased with the mischief we've wrought this day?

## THE EUROVISION SONG CONTEST – Some British entries that probably wouldn't go down too well

- Foreigners Are Scum (Doo Doo Doo)
- Europe Is a Pile of Shyte (Tiddle Pom)
- Rule Britannia (Britannia Rules the Waves)
- There'll Always Be an England (except when those federalist traitors sell us out, that is, tiddly pom, pom, pom)
- You All Stink, You Foreign Filth (La La La)
- Call That a Song, You Dago? (Ooh La La)
- The Ballad of Geoff Hurst
- We Shag Your Birds on Holiday (Tiddle Bing)
- Thank Christ for the Channel (Dingy-ding-ding)

- Up Yours, Jacques Santer! (repeated for 3 minutes 40 seconds)

## EUTHANASIA – Why it would be a godsend to the NHS

- It's cheaper to kill 'em than treat 'em
- The NHS can employ cheaper, less skilled surgeons with less steady hands
- Even junior doctors can perform euthanasia after 72 hours without sleep. They just can't go wrong!
- Fewer beds and nurses would be needed. You just wheel 'em in and kill 'em
- If someone pretending to be a doctor sneaked in, he could do the operation for free!
- Doctors wouldn't have to pretend that they cared any more
- Crematoria could be set up in the hospital grounds – and provide free hot water for the site
- Students could practise on patients with no fear of being sued
- The NHS has had lots of previous experience in killing patients
- They wouldn't need to buy any special equipment. All they'd have to do is shuttle the patient around between hospitals in an ambulance, searching for a spare bed

## THE FALKLANDS – Why it's time for a second Falklands war

- There's nothing on the telly
- The Argies have got better beef than we've got
- The squaddies in Cyprus are getting restless
- The *Sun*'s circulation figures are slipping
- We still haven't paid them back for Maradona's handball
- We're going to lose the next World Cup, so it would be nice to have something to cheer about
- Simon Weston wants to get his revenge
- New recruits to 3 Para are busting for an ear necklace
- If we lose a few frigates, maybe the shipyards can be reopened on the Tyne
- It's still a safe distance away


## FAMILY PLANNING CLINICS – Why they're an utter waste of time

- Who wants free condoms when you know they're just manufacturers' 'slight seconds'

- You can learn all you need to know about sex from any copy of *Penthouse*
- They don't allow you to 'practise' on any of the staff
- They're happy to give away free condoms but not boxes of Kleenex or tubes of KY and large vibrating phalluses
- The pictures in their literature are really tame compared with any porno mag you can buy in the high street
- If you tell them that you're not sure how to put a condom on they might start to snigger
- They're never open at 11.30 at night when you've got a bird back to your place who isn't on the Pill (and if they were they wouldn't deliver)

## FANTASIES – Politically Incorrect ones to have

- You are trapped on a desert island with Margaret Thatcher and a plank of wood with a nail knocked through it
- Any one that involves Lady Penelope
- Or the Little Mermaid
- Or Lady Penelope *and* the Little Mermaid
- You initiate a mind-swapping operation with Pamela Anderson and are caught. You are then thrown into solitary confinement in her body, with nothing but a mirror, a velvet glove and a large vibrating phallus for company. Meanwhile, your body, with Pamela's mind in it, is diagnosed as brain-dead and destroyed
- Finding out if Meg Ryan really does sound like that

## FAT CATS – Why chairmen of privatised utilities should earn a fortune

- If they didn't, there wouldn't be any incentive for middle management to work hard and strive for promotion

- It gives the Labour Party something to hark on about
- It's an incentive for shareholders to get off their arses and attend the AGM for once in their lives (with or without pig)
- If they didn't, they'd have to move out of their huge houses, depriving local authorities of much-valued Band H council tax
- It means they'll never go on strike for unfair pay
- It means they've got more to give to charity
- If they didn't, they wouldn't be respected by their colleagues, friends and families
- It enables the utilities to reduce their profits and therefore the amount of corporation tax they have to pay
- It gets the utilities in the tabloid press, raising their profile and attracting City interest
- They're too responsible to run through the streets waving their bulging wallets and yelling, 'Bet you wish this was yours, poor people!' (Except for Cedric Brown, that is, and it was only the once)

## FAT PEOPLE – Why they're incredibly stupid

- No fat person has ever been a nuclear physicist (they don't even make white lab coats bigger than a 42-inch chest)
- On average, they're 32 times more likely to join Weight Watchers than MENSA
- They're jolly, even when they're on the verge of a coronary
- They're more likely to have read the *Hip and Thigh Diet* than *A Brief History of Time* by Professor Stephen Hawking
- Anyone with a bum ten times the size of their head is not going to be gifted with too much up top
- Diet club meetings are known for their discussions about wholemeal bread and pulses, not stimulating arguments about existentialism

- Oliver Hardy might have known how to do a pratfall into a swimming pool but ask him to explain Sartre's concept of 'Being and Nothingness' and he was fucked!
- Fatty Arbuckle was the highest-paid entertainer in Hollywood – and he threw it all away
- Come on, who's smarter? Skinny Bamber Gascoigne – or his brother Paul 'Blubberguts' Gascoigne
- They've got fat heads
- *Vogue* magazine said they were

## FAT WOMEN – How to spot one

- She's fat
- Anywhere you go in a room, she's next to you
- Every time she wears high heels she strikes oil
- Every time she wants to take a dump she has to use a compass to find her arse
- The 'Talk Your Weight' machine shouts 'One at a time!'
- She goes to Dateline – and gets matched up with Birmingham
- You can tell how old she is by counting the rolls of fat
- From the back, you think the circus has come to town
- Greenpeace use her as a decoy for the Norwegian whaling fleet
- She buys her clothes from these fashion collections:
  'Snowdonia by the House of Moyet'
  'Blimp Girl de Paris'
  'Arbuckle of Mayfair'
  'Fergie Girl'
  'Blob by Pierre Montande'
  'Madame Plumpe de Grande'

## FATHER'S DAY – Why it should be scrapped

- Lots of people hate their dads and shouldn't have to waste their money
- It makes lots of working-class children feel left out
- They charge you £1.75 for a card with a badly painted Spitfire on the front and some crappy old doggerel so bad Ted Hughes might have written it
- Do they have a Son's Day? Fair's fair . . .
- You have to drive a hundred miles to see the old git, secure in the knowledge that he's already got the Super 8 projector out and is about to review your entire childhood
- You'll phone him up to wish him a happy Father's Day and he'll rant on for half an hour about how you shouldn't have called him because the telephone costs so much
- So he's your father; big deal . . .
- It's just a shallow commercial gimmick to let the Post Office get more money off you
- Every Father's Day, Cecil Parkinson sits around squirming
- Every Father's Day, Woody Allen sits around rubbing his hands with glee

## FEMALE CIRCUMCISION – Why it should be introduced to the West

- It would teach men who get their foreskin caught in their zip what pain is really about
- It would give us a chance to use the word *clitoridectomy* in everyday conversation (well, it makes a change from talking about sport or the weather)
- 40 million African women can't be wrong
- Anything that's demanded by Islam and endorsed by the Koran must be worth considering
- We have better hygiene standards, and the victim will have less chance of dying of septicaemia

84

- Lambeth Council are eager to appoint a Chief
  Ethnic Clitoridectomy Executive Officer – and
  they need a reason
- Fergie might go into hospital for an ingrowing
  toenail and have the wrong operation
- Adopting other cultures' traditions and customs
  broadens the mind (even though it might narrow
  the vagina)

## FEMALE IMPERSONATORS – What to do when you find that your son is secretly moonlighting as one

- Sit down and cry
- Sit down with him and have a long talk – and then
  cry.
- Sit down with him and have a long talk – then beat
  the living crap out of him
- Hide his 'falsies' just before he's due to go on stage
  and then flick V-signs at him from the audience
- Give him to Dr Bernardo's
- Move and don't tell him
- Offer to pay for the operation – and pray he never
  comes out from under the anaesthetic
- Change your will as quickly as possible
- Pray he wasn't that strange-looking bird you picked
  up at the club who gave you a blow-job

## FEMALE MPs – What they all have in common, Labour and Tory alike

- More than a passing resemblance to Oliver Reed
- The ability to crack walnuts with their thighs
- They shave twice a day to avoid five o'clock
  shadow
- More male hormones than Tony Blair
- More male hormones than Vinnie Jones
- They all look like Babe's love-child
- They're all on the Parliamentary Eyesore
  committee – as examples

- Every so often, you'll catch them eyeing up the ceremonial mace longingly
- The Queen likes to have them around because, when she opens Parliament, she gets all the wolf whistles, despite being 70
- None of them have ever been involved in any sex scandal whatsoever
- And if they had, no picture editor would be remotely interested in the negatives

## FILMS – 12 Politically Incorrect film sequels that are bound to be smash hits with the public

- RAMBO IV: South Central L.A. (This time he's out for Blood – and Crip)
- ALIENS IV: This time it's deportation
- TWO SINGLE WHITE FEMALES – in Love
- FRIDAY THE 13th PART 14: Jason Takes Battersea Dogs Home
- ET II: The Vivisection
- LETHAL WEAPON IV: Mel finally reveals why the series is called 'Lethal Weapon'
- REALLY INDECENT PROPOSAL
- BOB AND CAROL AND TED AND ALICE AND FIDO
- THE HUNT FOR RED OCTOBER II: In Julia Robert's Jacuzzi
- HONEY, I PUT THE KIDS IN CARE
- MISERY II: This time she's got Sting
- VERY BASIC INSTINCT

## THE FIRE SERVICE – Why it's a bad idea to allow women in the force

- They'd be too scared to slide down the pole in case they ladder their tights
- And if they did pluck up courage they'd spend all day sliding up and down it for sexual gratification, more than likely

- They'd be on the phone to their boyfriends all day, preventing people with emergencies from dialling in
- By the time they'd finished their make-up, the fire would be out
- The yellow helmets would mess up their hair
- And the respirators might smudge their lipstick
- They'd have fantasies about the gushing hose . . .
- If they entered a smoke-filled room they'd spend more time looking at the décor than they would for victims
- At the scene of a disaster they'd spend hours gossiping with policewomen and nurses

## FISHERMEN – What the EU would like us to do for Spanish fishermen

- Let them fish in our territorial waters
- Turn a blind eye to their illegal nets and fishing practises
- Kiss their oily butts on request
- Get in the water and sort of shoo our fish towards their nets
- Fetch them little bowls of tapas while they fish
- Mind their boats while they enjoy an afternoon siesta
- Bring donkeys out to them in little boats so they can do something traditional and mind-bogglingly bestial to them
- Go out into the fishing grounds on pedalos and shoo away the noisy seagulls for them
- Make washing illegal in Brixham, so when the Spanish trawlermen drop anchor, the place will smell like home
- Play flamenco all day on Radio 1 FM so they can tune in while they're fishing and not feel homesick
- Pretend they won the Armada, instead of getting hammered
- Lay off all our own trawlermen

## FOOTBALL PLAYERS – Why it's only just that they're paid more than nurses

- No one splashes out for a season ticket for Guy's or St Thomas'
- It takes more skill to hammer home a 40-yard volley than to administer a colostomy
- For 90 minutes on a Saturday afternoon, soccer players have to work *really*, *really* hard
- Football players have to train
- You don't see BSkyB and the BBC in a bidding war for the rights to screen Edgware General Hospital
- You couldn't get foreign players of the calibre of Cantona and Kanchelskis to cross the road for what an SRN earns
- People don't turn out in their thousands to stand in the rain and chant 'Come on you sisters!'
- If a soccer player makes a fatal mistake – by giving away a penalty – the entire nation turns on him. If a nurse makes a mistake, she only has to face the grieving relatives
- Soccer players have to drive balls through the tightest of defences; nurses only have to shave them
- Who'd want to play 'Subbuteo SRNs'?
- It would be stupid for Nike or Reebok to pay six-figure sums to a matron to advertise their trainers
- Soccer players are men; nurses are women

## FOREIGNERS – Some good fibs to tell tourists in London

- It is obligatory to haggle with taxi drivers over the fare
- It's considered good luck to tickle a Life Guard
- It's considered even better luck to tickle his horse
- The nearest tube station to Buckingham Palace is Grange Hill
- You can fish for salmon off Westminster Bridge
- The traditional term of address for a London policeman is 'wanker'

- A yellow line indicates free parking for one hour (a double yellow line indicates two hours)
- There is no speed limit on Victoria Embankment between midnight and 6 a.m.
- Windsor Castle is near Leicester Square
- In summer, nude sunbathing is permitted in only one of London's parks. This is St James's Park, off the Mall
- There's lots to do in Docklands

## FREE SPEECH – Why it's overrated

- Like most things that are free, it's not worth having

## FRIENDS OF THE EARTH – Why they aren't the Earth's *true* friends

- They hardly ever phone or write
- They don't send birthday cards
- They never invite the Earth to parties, stag nights or evenings down the pub with them
- They never fix the planet up on a blind date
- They never offer to help when the Earth is a bit hard up
- They see it every day, but never stop to talk
- They constantly walk all over it

## FRIENDS OF THE EARTH – 5 equally committed rival organisations

- Opponents of the Globe
- Antagonists of the Planet
- Foes of the World
- Opponents of the Sphere
- Adversaries of the Environment

## FRIGIDITY – Ways to recognise it in your girlfriend

- She says she 'doesn't feel like it'

- She refuses to dress up in those fisherman's waders and tutu you've just bought
- She says you don't satisfy her
- She doesn't want to try a three-in-a-bed with you and her best friend
- She doesn't want to try out that scene in the video 'Gang Bang-A-Go-Go'
- She doesn't want to do it when you stagger back from the Indian at 2 a.m. smelling of piss, lager and a Chicken Madras
- She doesn't want to do it without contraception
- She doesn't want to do it with her strapped to the bed
- She doesn't want you to take Polaroids of her naked to show your mates
- She claims she has a period (which is the same excuse she's used every month)

## FUNERALS – Politically Incorrect eulogies to make

- I'm sorry; but the man was a complete tosser. There you are . . .
- He hid his transvestite tendencies from his family to the very end
- What sort of man was George? Well . . . have you ever seen one of those big squishy black-and-orange slugs that comes out just after it's been raining . . .
- Between you and me, it's the first time he's been 'stiff' in 40 years! Boom, boom!
- To you, he was the perfect family man. Me, I always suspected he was the 'Salford Slasher'
- I said to him, I said, if you keep on wanking like this, it'll be the death of you . . .
- Cremation's too good for the likes of him!
- I think that finding out that his lovely wife, Virginia, had been sleeping with me for the past 22 years was what finally did him in . . .

- Fascist, ignoramus, Philistine, shite-talker, arsehole – yes, George was all these things, but so much more besides . . .
- Thank God he's snuffed it; let's *party*!

## FUNERALS – How to liven up the depressing church service

- Go 'Whhhhoooooooooooo!'
- Dress as the Grim Reaper and shout out, 'Who's next, fragile mortals?'
- Get out a ouija board
- Throw your voice saying, 'Help! Let me out! I can't breathe!'
- Demonstrate an impromptu magic trick – sawing the coffin in half
- Shout out, 'Burn in hell, you bastard'
- Shout out, 'Stop! Stop! I'm sure I could hear scratching noises'
- Drive a wooden stake through the coffin screaming, 'Take that, O creature of the night!!'
- Set off a wind-up laughing bag
- Expose yourself to grieving relatives
- Take bets on the will
- Pretend you're in the IRA and fire a rifle in the air

## FUR – Why it's perfectly acceptable to wear it

- Animals wear fur and no one complains
- Hundreds of minks died to make that coat and it would be a terrible waste if no one got genuine pleasure out of it
- Fur is a natural resource; it doesn't use up valuable limited resources like synthetics
- Minks are a renewable resource, just like renewable forests
- There is no cruelty – minks are often humanely drowned in a bucket before being skinned
- Making fur coats from animals is a positive environmental act – it's a form of recycling

- People stare at you in the street – making you feel like a movie star
- People gob at you in the street – reminding you of the great times you had as a teenager during the punk years
- Buying fur isn't an act of cruelty – the animal's already dead and skinned by the time you get it

**G-SPOT – 10 things that it is far more rewarding to find**

- One last can of lager tucked away right at the back of the fridge
- The phone number of that bird you met at the pub last night
- A toilet cubicle at a motorway service station that hasn't got piss all over the floor or a lone turd bobbing up and down in the bowl
- A busty hitchhiker with no boyfriend (or knickers)
- A pound coin and an old biro stuck under one of the sofa cushions
- Your boss slumped over his desk, clutching his heart
- A parking meter that's still got an hour left on it
- A spare packet of fags in the glove compartment of your car
- A girl that swallows
- Your way home after a stag night

**GOD – How we know without a doubt that He's white**

- Ancient religious sacrifices traditionally involved goats or sheep, not chicken gumbo or black-eyed peas

- Not one hymn contains the phrases 'Get on down!' or 'Move on up (y'all)!'
- His son Jesus is traditionally portrayed as looking more like Robert Powell than Colin Powell
- The Song of Solomon is not a rap
- When Moses came down from Mount Sinai after talking to God he didn't greet Aaron with 'Hey, bro', gimme five!'
- God enabled Jesus to walk on water, not moon-walk
- When the Israelites wandered in the wilderness God sent them manna from heaven – not watermelon
- The Ten Commandments were chiselled into stone – not spray-painted
- In the Bible it doesn't say, 'And on the seventh day he body-popped'
- Jesus's followers were known as disciples – not his posse
- Jesus treated Mary Magdalene with respect – and didn't add her to his 'stable of ho's'
- In not one of Blake's religious paintings does God look remotely like Huggy Bear
- Noah was told by God to construct a huge ark from gopher wood – not a BMW with tinted windows, alloys and a 'jumpin' sound system'
- He allowed Abraham Lincoln and Martin Luther King to be assassinated

### GAMBLING – Why it's better to be a gambler than a rabbi

- Kenny Rogers will write a cracking good song about you
- Las Vegas is far more fun than Golders Green
- It's hard to cheat at religion
- Baccarat is more fun than sitting Shiva

- Gamblers always have a glamorous moll draped around their neck. A prayer shawl isn't nearly so arousing
- It's easier to study your opponent's face than the Talmud
- Luck is a lady; God's an old man with a beard
- Rabbis seldom, if ever, get a cool nickname like 'Lucky', 'Ace' or 'Full Flush Pete'
- It's hard to indulge your James Bond fantasies in a synagogue
- If you're a gambler, you can break the bank. If you're a rabbi, the bank seems like it's out to break you
- Gamblers are seldom if ever called upon to preside over a circumcision
- A rabbi has all his chips on just one number

## GANDHI – Things he was a complete and utter failure at

- Winning 'The Best Dressed Man of the Year' award
- Preventing chronic hair loss
- Ever coming first in a 'Drink Your Own Piss' contest, despite numerous attempts
- Completing the Charles Atlas course he sent away for
- Wearing a trendy pair of specs
- Kung fu
- Wearing a toupee without getting a big laugh
- Telling jokes no one had heard before
- Avoiding being mistaken for Alf Garnett
- Auditioning for the role of Rhett Butler in *Gone with the Wind*
- Rollerblading
- Sumo wrestling
- Achieving long-term peace in the Indian sub-continent

## GAY VICARS – Why they shouldn't be allowed

- The vicar's wife might be called Colin – or Gregory
- They might fancy Jesus
- They might fancy God
- If you sing 'Lord of the Dance', they might start voguing
- How could you be sure that, under their priest's clothes, their nipples weren't pierced?
- They'll bring in two good friends from Camden to redecorate the church with 'warmer, more touchy-feely colours'
- They surely couldn't be asked to judge the traditional village marrow-growing contest . . .
- They might giggle when they ask you to kneel
- The Eucharist wafer would be home-baked with just a touch of turmeric and oregano

## GAYS – Why we shouldn't allow gays in the armed forces

- The admirals would never get a stroke of work done
- The generals wouldn't commit their troops for fear of blemishing their handsome young toy boys' David-esque features
- They'll spend hours rag-rolling their tanks
- Voguing into battle is distracting for other troops in the field
- The Queen's Own Highlanders are bound to attract the wrong sort
- It's off-putting to think there might be a bender about while you're squatting over a bourbon biscuit with your mates, seeing who's the last to ejaculate on it
- It's disturbing to think there might actually be gay men about when squaddies are initiating some new recruit by stuffing objects up his arse

- They just wouldn't fit in. (It's hard to imagine them raping and killing women in Cyprus, for example . . .)

## GENESIS – Why it's Politically Incorrect

- It's sexist (portraying a woman as a temptress)
- It's speciesist (portraying a serpent as evil)
- Its explanation of creating a woman from a man's rib suggests that women are no more than an appendage
- There's no alternative to heterosexual love
- God is referred to as male (when we all know 'She' looks like Bea Arthur)
- The bit about the apple is fruitist
- Eve's fascination with the serpent perpetuates the evil myth of penis envy
- It says that God looked upon his work and saw that it was good – which is a blatant value judgement
- There are no black people, single mothers or Irish-Somali lesbians with learning difficulties anywhere in the story (well, not in our Bible, anyway)

## GENTLEMEN'S CLUBS – Why it's right that women should be excluded

- Men are excluded from the Women's Institute
- There are no ladies' toilets
- Unless they smoke cigars and drink brandy all day they'd feel left out
- They'll be bored since the only publications in the reading room tend to be *Wisden's Cricketer's Almanac*, *Cricket Monthly* and *What Bail?*
- They wouldn't be able to join in such stimulating discussions about cricket, cricket and, er . . . cricket
- The older members might have heart attacks and if a lot of company chairmen die, it won't be good for share prices

- Women aren't really able to wear the Club tie
- Men who have had nothing whatsoever to do with women in their first 60 years certainly don't want to start now
- If women were allowed to join, gentlemen's clubs would have to be known as gentlepersons' clubs, which would sound silly

## GHETTO SLANG – An example of how it can be made much more Politically Correct

- Yo, female pet companion! Yo, sex care provider! Get your significant female other with powerful matriarchal connections with whom a non-oppressive non-phallocentric sexual relationship is being mutually enjoyed ass into my car! My male phallic instrument of repression is throbbing for your female positive expression of wimmin's vulvic superiority! Hey, you intellectually challenged melanin-enriched person of African-American extraction, are you audially different?

## GINGER HAIR – terms of endearment for people with this terminal condition

- Carrot Head
- Fergie Clone
- Ginge the Minge
- Rusty Bonce
- Orange Noodle
- Middle Traffic Light Head
- Ferric Oxide Cranium
- Rufus Twat
- Tangerine Top
- Satsuma Thatch
- Tango Dome
- My Darling Clementine
- That Twat Chris Evans

## GLASS CEILING – Why it's there

- To stop women taking your job
- To give mediocre men some chance of making it in life
- A concrete ceiling would be too obvious

- As would a ceiling with 'no women beyond this point' painted on it
- It ensures you don't lose your invaluable PA who really does your job for you
- Women can't play golf for toffee
- So that, even if they do get promoted over you, you can still lean your head back and see up their skirts
- So that other women can be paid £1.50 an hour to clean and polish it after work

## GLUE SNIFFING – Why it's good

- It's not as antisocial as smoking
- It's cheap enough not to have kids stealing to maintain their habit
- It's better than 'turd sniffing'
- It prevents kids from progressing straight on to adult drugs, which might be too much of a shock to their system
- It's a necessary diversion from schoolwork
- When your older brother dies with his head in a plastic bag you get his room and CD collection
- It's usually practised by morons and the world could get by quite easily with a few less garage mechanics
- You can make an Airfix Lysander and get high at the same time
- You can shrink-fit your new 501s by pissing in them while under the influence

## GOOD FAIRY – Some other positive gay role models for kids

- Roger the Magic Interior Designer
- Pixie Pam, the Lesbian Leprechaun
- Gregory, the Gay who Saved Christmas
- Gina and Tina, the Diesel Dyke Donkeys
- Vincent the Voguing Vegan
- The Easter Transvestite
- Teenage Mutant Ninja Hairdressers

- Mighty Morphin Flower Arrangers
- Barney

## GRAFFITI – Why it's definitely not a proletarian art form

- A proletarian art form is a contradiction in terms
- Drawing a huge penis and a pair of bollocks takes relatively little skill and perception
- Spray-painting 'Gaz' on the side of a tube train does not enrich the lives of all those who experience it
- Writing 'Jane Smith is a syphy dog with genital warts' on a wall will not ensure you a place on a school English syllabus in ten years' time (or perhaps it will)
- Writing 'Wayne 4 Karen Tru' provides you with little insight into the human condition
- No art critic ever goes up to London Regional Transport managers and says, 'I'll give you a million pounds for that exquisitely graffiti-ed carriage'
- 'Tits!' written somewhere at random has never been reviewed by a broadsheet newspaper for its literary merit
- There is not one single copy of the famous 'Clapham Posse' tag hanging in any art gallery in the world
- Only the most liberal of politically correct gits would think that the word 'Wanker' painted in large black letters on a railway bridge should be preserved for posterity
- If graffiti were a genuine art form, people from all over the world would be flocking to the South Mimms service station toilets, and they would rival Florence as destination number one for the true aesthete (instead of destination number one for burly lorry drivers who like to scrawl obscenities during a marathon dump)

## GRAMMAR SCHOOLS – Why we should bring them back

- They can't be worse than comprehensives
- So that stupid children can go to secondary moderns and learn useful skills, like how to overcharge on plumbing estimates and where the distributor cap is on a Ford Fiesta
- Labour politicians won't have to send their children out of the borough any more
- Children will no longer have the lowest common denominator applied to them
- Children will actually know what 'lowest common denominator' means
- You get a better class of knifing incident in a grammar school
- Your children are more likely to do coke than crack
- Brighter children will be more likely to know the sweet smell of success rather than the sickly-sweet smell of glue
- Children with IQs of 120-plus will no longer share the classroom with Neanderthals who can't write their names in the ground with a stick
- So teachers would have no excuse for being such failures

## GRANDMOTHERS – 8 Politically Incorrect designs for their 85th birthday cake

- A V-1 flying bomb, just like the one that destroyed her home and all her possessions in 1944
- Her cat, lying prostrate in a sponge gutter with the chocolate tyre-track marks of an eighteen-wheeler going over its head, tastefully decorated with lots of raspberry jam
- A sponge cake in the shape of a medal bearing the inscription 'Champion NHS Sponger'
- A gravestone with her name on it, finished off with a flourish of pink icing saying 'Soon'

- A giant penis with Hundreds and Thousands for pubes and marzipan for the big blue vein
- An hourglass (use those tiny silver balls to represent the sand – nearly all of it should be at the bottom)
- The wreckage of a Hawker Hurricane, just like the one in which her darling husband plunged to his doom in the Romney Marshes
- A gigantic turd, covered in 85 candles

## GREEN PARTY – 11 causes the politically ignorant might expect it to represent

- Swarfega
- Mouldy Sandwich Spread
- Phlegm after a heavy cold
- Avocados
- People that are seasick
- Broccoli
- Chlorophyll
- Emeralds
- Gangrene
- Bogies
- Frogs

## GREEN PARTY – Sex scandals we can expect to see if one of their MPs ever gets elected

- Three-in-a-bed sex romp with a cauliflower and a Brussels sprout
- Having an affair with a 22-year-old potato
- Being photographed in a compromising position with soya
- Being caught on Hampstead Heath, trying to proposition a shrub
- Kerb-crawling outside the Royal Horticultural Show
- Leaving their wife and family for a plate of soya
- Checking into a Brighton hotel with a rather attractive courgette
- Being caught at an orgy in Kew Gardens
- Being found dead with an orange in their mouth
- Trying to lure a young sapling into an alleyway with a bag of mulch

**GREENPEACE – Why they should forget about whaling and instead strive for international bans on the following:**

- Old people driving
- Old people living
- Large-breasted girls wearing baggy clothing
- Shell suits
- Fat people
- News about the Royal Family
- The Royal Family
- Caravans
- Short people
- Anyone with a car better than yours
- Quorn
- Anthea Turner

**GREENPEACE SHIPS – Why they all need to be sunk**

- They play ambient music at all hours of the night and keep the fish awake
- They are painted horrible bright colours, which makes the dolphins feel queasy
- Sinking them helps to keep the French secret service in proper combat readiness
- When they settle on the sea bed, coral will form over them and a beautiful new reef will be born
- All hippies must drown

**GULF WAR SYNDROME – Why the MOD should ignore claims for compensation**

- Just because the US Government admits it exists doesn't mean to say that it does
- You don't hear the Iraqi forces complaining (well, the ones that survived, anyway)
- If you go abroad, you expect the odd gyppy tummy
- It's a convenient excuse for ex-squaddies to laze about at home on sickness benefit watching horseracing and drinking beer

- It is impossible to prove brain damage in most squaddies
- Jim Macdonald from *Coronation Street* served in the British Army and he didn't suffer from it
- Where would it stop? WWI veterans claiming 'Ypres Syndrome'? Or families of dead soldiers retrospectively claiming 'Waterloo Syndrome'?
- If the MOD had to pay millions of pounds in compensation, they wouldn't have enough money for planes or tanks to fight the next Gulf War and our troops would have to go into battle armed with sharp sticks

## FORREST GUMP – Why life really is like a box of chocolates

- It's expensive
- It's stale
- You wish someone had given you the Bendicks mints instead of the caramelised oranges
- Most of it is just air and fancy packaging
- You know the person giving it to you didn't give it much thought
- Those with soft centres are easily squashed
- The greedy take a handful
- There are too many nuts
- You end up feeling sick
- At the end of the day, you're left with the dregs
- It seems like it's finished in five minutes

## GYNAECOLOGISTS – Insensitive (and unprofessional) things to say during an 'internal'

- 'Spread 'em, darlin' '
- 'Yodel-odel-oooooh! Wow! Listen to that echo'
- 'Open wide!'
- 'Smile! You're on *Candid Camera*'
- 'Fancy a quick one?'
- 'Eurrrggghhhh! Are you allergic to soap or what?!'

- 'Have you heard that song "How Deep Is Your Love"?'
- 'Now I know what it's like being sucked into a black hole'
- 'It's like the *Lusitania* down here – full of dead seamen'
- 'I'm going in. Keep me covered!'
- 'You don't need a gynaecologist, lady, you need Dyno-Rod'
- 'Phworrrrrrr!'

## GYPSIES – 12 mystic things that all true gypsies instinctively know

- Where the nearest lead roofing is
- How to circumvent council regulations
- How to have sixteen children, all of whom seem about the same age
- How to breed the ugliest, greasiest, most savage mongrel dogs
- How to fit four packets of cornflakes and a bottle of Lambrusco inside a leather bomber jacket
- Every fairground, carnival, fête and horse show in the country
- Every fairground, carnival, fête and horse show con, scam, sharp practice and racket going
- How to get the most from the DSS
- How to break down a Ford Fiesta for spares
- How to turn four acres of pristine grass verge into a huge rubbish tip
- Which pillock is most likely to buy a sprig of 'lucky heather'
- How to afford a £20,000 caravan and an H-reg Jag on social security benefits

## GYPSIES – One thing that no gypsy knows

- How to maintain the Mighty Waltzer safely

## HAMBURGER CHAINS – Why it's good they're clearing the rainforests to make more room to graze cattle

- Once you've seen one tree, you've seen them all
- Ditto endangered species
- Ditto tribes of funny brown folk
- It's a bugger to sweep up the forest floors come autumn
- If they didn't clear them, the cows would bang into the trees, hurting their heads
- It's better than clearing the towns and cities
- It's a more effective way of getting rid of poisonous snakes and spiders than stomping around wearing big boots
- It provides welcome employment for Brazilian bulldozer drivers
- And petty arsonists
- Most people in the West value burgers over some rare orchid that *might* provide a cure for cancer (some day)
- The cows are about as far away from BSE-infested Britain as you can get

## HAMBURGERS – Why they're much better than 'healthy' vegetarian food

- You don't get a free plastic kids' toy with a lentil nut cutlet
- You can eat a hamburger while you're driving; try doing that with a vegetable moussaka
- The person who serves you always says something pleasant like 'Have a nice day' – not something like 'Will we see you at the neo-Marxist potato and carrot growers' co-operative next week?'
- There's absolutely no preparation involved
- Or washing up
- Burger chains guarantee that their polystyrene packaging is made without CFCs; who knows what dangerous polymers are concealed within a leek and potato pie?
- When you've finished, it's socially acceptable to drop your leftovers on the pavement; try doing that with a plate of cauliflower and mushroom flan
- Children are more likely to be entertained by a jolly clown character than they are by the frankly morose Linda McCartney
- Fast-food joints are convenient, but vegetarians are too stuck up to open a 'McTurnips', 'Asparagus King', 'Kentucky Fried Lentil', 'Pulse-U-Like' or 'Marrow Hut'
- Even the manky bit of dill pickle they put on top of burgers is a hundred times tastier than anything vegetarian

## HANGING – Why it *shouldn't* be brought back

- It's too good for them

## HARD-CORE PORN FILMS – Why they're bad for you

- They make you insanely jealous; you know you'll never ever get to do it with three blondes and a snake

- Arthritis in the wrist in later life can be particularly painful
- Until now, you didn't realise how small yours was . . .
- Or how lop-sided
- You can only watch the movie at four in the morning when your wife is fast asleep and you're ruined at work the next day
- All the great chat-up lines you learn from the films, like 'Hey, bitch, suck on this', just don't seem to work in real life
- You get so disappointed when the next caller at your door isn't some busty young sex aid salesgirl who's just split up with her boyfriend
- You think that the 'shaven' look is sexy – and then make the mistake of splashing on some aftershave . . .
- It's always the porno tape that's jammed in your machine when you have to call in the man from Radio Rentals
- You invariably put the video on by mistake when you want to show your parents your holiday in Madeira
- You get all these great new ideas for sex from the films – and then your missus slaps you and makes you throw them all out

## HIGH COURT JUDGES – Why it's good that they're really, really old

- If they weren't, they wouldn't have a valid excuse for being so out of touch with the public
- If they make a terrible mistake, like releasing a killer back into society, they don't have long to live with it on their conscience
- People will automatically put any bad judgements down to Alzheimer's disease
- They get a free wig to cover their baldness

- When they're arrested for soliciting prostitutes (and/or rent boys) it's not worth the courts giving them a prison sentence because they'll die before completing it
- They can justify a really lenient jail sentence by claiming that 'in their day, before decimalisation and centimetres and things, six months was worth a lot more . . .'
- They're able to remain totally unshocked in cases involving child abuse, sex crimes or racial attacks because they don't understand the concepts
- It gives employment to people who would otherwise have been written off as geriatrics
- They soon die and make room for other, nearly as old High Court judges

## HOME EDUCATION – How to simulate your child's education at home

- To simulate classroom size, take your child to a busy railway station thronging with commuters. Put him on platform one. Go to platform three and then shout the principles of algebra to him
- Call him fat, useless and a 'big girl' to simulate a real-life PE lesson
- Say you're going to play football at playtime – then don't pick him for your team
- Instead of cooking him dinner, give him a lunchbox with a pork pie, an apple and a Kit-Kat, along with a thermos full of strawberry Nesquik that rattles rather suspiciously . . .
- Take him up to the toilet, lock yourselves in and share a fag
- Fall asleep in front of the telly, to simulate the headmaster's interest in your child
- Tell him you'll sell him a rock of crack for his dinner money
- Bully your child until he has a nervous breakdown, then complain to yourself and do nothing about it

- Meet your child at the garden gate and kick him until he cries
- Put your child in a class with your cat and the washing up. Hold him back until all three can achieve equal grades

## THE HOMELESS – How to wind them up

- Go up to one and say, 'I'm an estate agent and that box is worth £50,000. Interested?'
- Superglue the locks on all the temporary Christmas shelters
- Approach someone sleeping in a box and show them a Polaroid of your semi
- Tell someone huddled in a doorway that there's a Salvation Army soup kitchen just around the corner. As soon as they go, steal all their blankets
- Tell them with a smile and a wink that you voted Conservative in the last election
- Invite them to come and stay with you – then give them the slip on the train
- Superglue a pound coin to the pavement
- Take a slash in a shop doorway and then say, 'Oh, sorry. I didn't see you there . . .'
- Sit around one of their fires, share their food and booze and cigarettes, then look at your watch and say that it's time to go home to your penthouse suite now
- Whistle appreciatively and say, 'Hey! Nice rags!'
- Go up to them and say, 'Hello, I'm your local Conservative MP. I trust I can count on your vote in the next election.' Run.
- Go round the local dossers' hangout with a wheely-bin calling, 'Mobile home for sale!'
- Flaunt your MIRAS certificate
- Invent a new type of Monopoly where players buy different-value cardboard boxes
- Go up to a shop doorway at night and say, 'Excuse me, are you queueing for the Debenhams sale?'

- Pretend you're making a documentary about people *with* homes and tell them that they can't be in it
- Get a load of friends pretending to be double glazing salesmen to pester them. When they get pissed off say, 'Now you know what it feels like to own a house!'
- Ask them what council tax band their cardboard box is in

## THE HOMELESS – What we really need to give them apart from a roof over their heads

- A Brillo pad and a bar of Lifebuoy
- Steam cleaning with liquid Mum
- Delousing
- Two passes through a sheep dip
- Submerging in a vat full of Dettol
- Sand blasting
- Four litres of Wash 'n' Go
- Two or three hundred revolutions in a tumble dryer on cycle eight
- A wide berth

## THE HOMELESS – Why they're lucky bastards

- They don't have to pay council tax
- They don't have to pretend to be out when the man comes to read the gas meter
- Or the electricity meter
- They don't have to bother about repainting the windows or repositioning the TV aerial
- They don't have to put up with noisy neighbours with screaming kids
- They're safe in the knowledge that their wives aren't having affairs with the milkman or window cleaner
- They don't have to give bastard children sweets at Halloween
- Or the bastard dustmen a fiver at Christmas

- They don't have double glazing circulars or Oxfam and Christian Aid envelopes littering the doormat
- People don't park across their driveways
- They don't have to buy new batteries for the doorbell
- They don't have to worry about burglars
- Or the extortionate cost of house contents insurance
- They don't have to put the cat out at night
- They don't lie awake at night worrying about the cost of endowment mortgages, negative equity and the ever-present threat of repossession . . .

## HOMEOPATHY – Some equally effective 'alternative' treatments for ailments

- Irritable Bowel Syndrome – Dance naked around the boundaries of Chelmsford while being thrashed with empty packets of Angel Delight
- Arthritis – Have your head nailed to a meringue
- Slipped Disc – Hold your breath for seven minutes while your face is painted like a clown's
- Athlete's Foot – Eat nothing but rhubarb and watch nothing but *Home and Away* for six months, while hanging upside down from the ceiling
- Tennis Elbow – Drink one-third Guinness, two-thirds Liebfraumilch while chewing sugar-free gum and sticking rusty safety pins in the back of your neck
- Impotence – Rub fresh cat pooh in your hair and shop in Tesco's
- Earache – Drive your car at eighty miles an hour dressed as a Red Indian, with Simply Red on the stereo
- Toothache – Consume half a pint of stale dog vomit and bang your head repeatedly against a wall
- Sore Nipples – Tie your arms to the back of a Eurojuggernaut and get dragged for in excess of 100 miles on your face

- Hernia – Make it up yourself; it really doesn't matter

## HOMOSEXUALITY – Why it's OK

- All the more women for us (except, probably, for the gay ones)!
- Poor rent boys would go hungry otherwise
- While the police are persecuting gays, other minorities get a breather
- It allows all manner of cheap gay jokes and *double entendres*
- What's good enough for the Royals is good enough for us

## HOMOSEXUALS – Why they should be welcomed into the armed forces with open arms

- They already know three ways to kill a man just using their little finger (all of them quite pleasurable)
- They'd never be reprimanded for keeping an untidy barracks
- It's more than likely that someone who can knock up a crème brûlée in ten minutes would be able to reassemble a rifle in the dark
- Their experiences on Hampstead Heath will come in useful for cross-country night manoeuvres
- Their experiences in applying eye liner will come in useful when applying camouflage paint
- 'Cottaging' will give them a head start in covert operations
- Being a 'Brown Hatter' sounds like it isn't a million miles removed from being a 'Green Beret' (according to military gossip)
- Similarly, lying down with your fellow soldier isn't that far from laying down your life for your fellow soldier
- They're used to watching each others' backs

- They might not be straight but they can shoot and march that way
- If they're posted abroad they'll be so busy visiting the local art galleries and shopping that they won't have time to get pissed out of their heads and assault and kill Danish tour guides

## HONG KONG – Why we don't want any of its residents over here in 1997

- We have more than enough takeaways
- Just because they invented writing, paper, gunpowder and government – and built the only man-made object that can be seen from space – they think they're smarter than us
- They've all got exactly the same name and newspaper deliveries would be very confusing
- They'll give Burma veterans horrific flashbacks
- They all know kung fu
- Opticians will need to retool
- One of them might be Fu Manchu
- They might all jump off their chairs at the same time and the Isle of Wight will sink
- Chinatown will be the size of Devon
- Boots the Chemist will have to start stocking Panda Penis and Tiger Goolies
- There's only so much laundry that needs doing
- If they wanted to practise the Chinese water torture on each other, they couldn't because of all our drought orders
- They'd probably hold pro-democracy rallies, which our government wouldn't like
- *The Chinese Detective* will be number one in the TV ratings forever and ever and ever

## HOUSEHOLD CHORES – Why women should do them

- They've had more practice
- They know all the latest gadgets and cleaners, because they're advertised on daytime TV

- Aprons are designed for women
- Women know where all the messy cooking spills are – because they made them
- Most surfaces that need cleaning are at just the right height for a woman
- Men don't know one end of a duster from the other
- Men feel demeaned and their masculinity suffers
- Household chores don't require any skill
- Being shorter, women don't have to bend down so far to dust in corners
- They've been blessed with the vacuuming gene

## HOUSING ESTATES – 17 things you'll never, ever find there

- A library card
- A twelve-year-old virgin
- A car with a tax disc
- A family that's not known to the police
- Conservative Party canvassers
- A dog that isn't at least one half pit bull
- A VCR with a receipt
- Someone without a tattoo
- A home without a Simply Red cassette
- A four-year-old who doesn't know the word 'fuck'
- Someone whose rent is paid up to date
- Someone without a county court judgement against them
- Someone who doesn't know someone with a Transit
- Prince Andrew on the pull
- Peace and quiet
- Spiritual fulfilment
- Hope

## HOUSING ESTATES – One thing you'll be certain of finding there

- Sky dishes

**THE INDIAN SUB-CONTINENT – Its 17 most important contributions to the Western world**

- Delhi Belly
- Lahore Looseness
- Bangalore Bowels
- Karachi Cork
- Tamil Two Step
- Goa Gallops
- Calcutta's Curse
- Vishnu's Voiding
- Tripura Trots
- Rawalpindi Runs
- Shiva Squirts
- Hyderabad Hop
- Rama's Revenge
- Ganges Gastroenteritis
- Rangoon Rear
- Chittagong Shitalong
- Shops that stock over 38 different pornographic magazines

**INDUSTRY – How we can all support British industry**

- Support a favourite company like ICI or Plessey
- Turn up and cheer it on at the AGM or Stock Exchange
- Get together with your mates and beat up rival supporters who follow Eastern Electricity or Mercury
- Paint your face in the company colours
- Compose songs like 'Who's That Wanker in the Monopolies and Mergers Commission?'
- Watch Frank and David in *Fantasy Industry* on TV
- Have the logo tattooed on your arm – or your forehead
- Name your son after the entire board of directors
- Follow your favourite company on trade delegations abroad
- Set up fanzines like *When Monday Comes*

**INFORMATION – Why it's useless as the new currency**

- You can't exchange it for 3,000 pesetas for your holiday in Benidorm
- Likewise, you can't buy 200 Rothmans with it at Malaga airport
- No prostitute will give you 'half and half' in exchange for two facts and a supposition
- How would you like to be paid in theoretical discourses?
- No one will give you credit against a fact
- Anyone who read the *Encyclopaedia Britannica* would automatically become a billionaire
- Anyone who read the *Sun* would become bankrupt
- You can't stand a round with a wallet full of data
- A little knowledge is a dangerous thing – especially if payday is still three days away

## INSOMNIACS – How to make life worse for them

- Show them the latest burglary figures
- Tell them you've heard rumours that they're next for the chop at work
- Lend them a really creepy video
- Ask why you saw their partner driving somewhere at five yesterday morning
- Tell them you've heard that counting sheep doesn't work, but counting ways you could lose a limb does . . .
- Ask them how they think they'll die
- Tell them that most people die in their sleep
- Lend them a copy of *Invasion of the Body Snatchers* and then leave a giant seed pod next to their bed
- Tell them that their house has a reputation for being the most haunted house in Britain

## INSURANCE – Things you should insure against now

- The Tories being in power when you retire
- Your life assurance being no good, because the stock market crashed and wiped it out
- Your life assurance being no good, because some bastard company director stole it
- Your life assurance being no good, because 97.5% went in 'fees'
- Your life assurance being no good, because Bangladesh never became a 'tiger economy' (in fact it sank in 2002)
- Your life assurance being no good, because the economy collapsed and the only recognised currencies of exchange are shotgun shells and canned foods
- Your life assurance being no good, because the government of the day plans to tax it at 99%
- Your pension being £200 a week – but a tea bag costs £40,000

## INTELLIGENCE IN ANIMALS – Why it's a myth

- There are no three-toed sloths in MENSA
- A wombat has yet to make it through to even the qualifying rounds of *The Krypton Factor*
- Name one animal who has ever made a scientific breakthrough (by itself, as opposed to having 40,000 volts shot up its bum)
- If antelope had any sense, they'd arm themselves against lions
- No fish has ever published a book on philosophy
- A chimp has succeeded in outwitting Jim Davidson on more than one occasion – but that by itself proves nothing . . .
- Animals work in experimental labs every day – but they never think of quitting the job
- Animals going to a slaughterhouse know they're going to be killed, but they don't try to make a run for it

## INTERIOR DESIGN – 8 things every true man should have in his living room

- A carpet that looks like an incontinent panicked wildebeest has traversed it
- A library (two Sven Hassel books from a jumble sale, the Haynes XR3i manual, a copy of *How to be a Complete Bastard* complete with wee-wee splashes, *Zen and the Art of Motorcycle Maintenance* (bought in error))
- Litter bin (contents: fourteen empty cans of Special Brew, eight empty packets of B&H, chewed-up video cassette, remains of last week's Chinese takeaway)
- Carpet stain where you dropped your chicken curry and trod all over it in a drunken delirium last night
- Videos (the collected works of Sylvester Stallone, plus a smattering of soccer, kickboxing and rally sports tapes, and that Pinky and Perky tape your mates got you for a laugh on your birthday)

- More videos (pervy and ultra-pervy tapes, bought from the proverbial 'man in a pub'. Two-thirds are completely blank, while one is so distorted it could be *Nymphos in Heat* – or equally it could be *Inspector Morse*
- Windows and ceiling encrusted with enough nicotine to make a whole pack of beagles keel over
- And down the back of the sofa – the car keys you've been desperately trying to find, 35½p in loose change, five socks, eight Callard & Bowser wrappers, a *TV Times* from 1987, the toenail scissors (which you've long since given up for lost, having resorted to using the kitchen ones instead), half a spring roll and a prawn cracker, a leaky ballpoint, a crushed Special Brew can, two knives, a fork, a teaspoon, a rolled-up *Fiesta*, that tube of Preparation H you hid when that girl came back to your flat that time, fifteen ring-pulls, and enough dirt to put Robert Maxwell's financial dealings to shame

## INTERIOR DESIGN – 14 things every true man should have in his kitchen

- Filth
- Dirt
- Grime
- Grease
- Charring from the one time he tried to cook for himself and the chip pan caught fire
- Bacteria seldom seen outside of sewage treatment farms
- Bacteria *never* seen outside of sewage treatment farms
- A crusty puddle where he threw up in 1990, but was too drunk to remember it the next morning
- More washing up to do than the whole of Trust House Forte gets through in a year

- A mould culture that would excite professional mould-ologists the world over if they could only see it
- Dirty socks, unaccountably left on work surface (to help it smell better?)
- Cornflakes so old there's a free plastic Captain Scarlet action figure at the bottom
- A J-cloth that looks, feels and smells like it's been dead for a hundred years
- Underwear soaking in washing-up bowl

## THE INTERNET – Why we don't need it

- If we wanted to talk to sad and lonely inadequates, we could go trainspotting
- If we wanted to read semi-literate ridiculous sexual fantasies, it's cheaper to buy a copy of *Forum Readers' Letters*
- If we wanted to have a heart-stopping phone bill at the end of the quarter, we could ring up live sex chat lines – or get a mobile
- If we wanted to meet paedophiles we could just as easily go along to a local council-run care home
- In the time it takes to download Stephen Hawking's home page, we could have reinvented his entire life's work (and understood it)
- If we wanted to log on to a remote camera in a New York car wash we should get a life
- If we wanted to exchange views on current affairs with a load of other morons we'd go down the pub
- If we wanted to lie about our appearance to women, we'd stuff a ten-inch courgette down our pants
- If we really wanted to know every single continuity error in every episode of *Star Trek*, *Next Generation*, *Deep Space 9* and *Voyager*, it would be better if we took an overdose and put ourselves out of our misery

- If we wanted to fill our hard disk with a load of boring shite we'd load a copy of *Double Entry Bookkeeping for Windows* (that or some interactive encyclopaedia about castles)
- If we wanted to contribute to the unbelievable profits made by BT we'd become a shareholder first

## THE IRA – Why it's better to fight in the IRA than in the British Army

- You get to wear a black balaclava, so after duty you can play at being a trainspotter (or a rapist)
- It's far more romantic being known as a 'freedom fighter' than a 'squaddie'
- You get invited to loads of funerals where you can fire your gun (and tuck into the sausage rolls afterwards)
- If you get arrested you can lose a few unsightly pounds by going on a hunger strike
- Or express yourself artistically by smearing your shit all over your prison cell
- You can operate a 'shoot to kill' policy and no one complains
- Or refers you to the European courts
- You can kneecap who you like
- If you shoot someone you get to be a hero; if you're in the Army and you shoot someone, you get to go to jail . . .
- 'Danny Boy' is a more stirring song to sing than 'Four and Twenty Virgins'
- In the Army all you do is defuse bombs; in the IRA you get to make them
- In the regular Army you get to go to some real dumps like Belize or the Falklands. In the IRA you make regular trips to the United States
- If you go against orders in the British Army you're arrested and court-martialled. In the IRA you're just known as a 'splinter group'

- If you *are* arrested, it's better to be a 'political prisoner' than just a 'prisoner'
- It's far safer attacking a civilian target than it is a military one

## THE IRISH – Why Americans are so keen to claim Irish descent

- They can get pissed on St Patrick's Day
- Other people make allowances for them
- It helps them to explain why they're still junior clerks in their late forties
- They can be chronic alcoholics and people just say, 'Oh, he's a good ol' boy'
- People make allowances for their appalling carrot-coloured hair, noses like Karl Malden and bad complexions
- They can talk complete and utter bollocks and fellow Americans will just shrug and say, 'It's the blarney in him' . . .
- It helps rude and obnoxious people seem charming somehow
- It's better than claiming Polish descent

## IRRITABLE BOWEL SYNDROME – Other terms for this condition

- Grumbly Rectum Condition
- Cantankerous Colon Disease
- Ill-Humoured Anal Malady
- Petulant Bum Complaint
- Peevish Proctorial Predicament
- Tense Back Passage Virus
- Cross Botty Sickness
- Fretful Anus Upset
- Irascible Bumhole Ailment
- Fucking Pissed Off Sphincter Affliction

## ISLAMIC FUNDAMENTALISM – Why it's fifty times better than Hare Krishna

- It's more fun shouting abuse outside the American embassy than it is chanting to yourself
- Likewise, it's far more satisfying beating a Western hostage than it is a tambourine
- You don't have to shave your hair off and look like that bloke from Right Said Fred
- Or the Tango man
- Being a suicide bomber takes more courage than walking down Oxford Street dressed like a stupid giant tangerine
- You're more likely to find Salman Rushdie than you are enlightenment
- Burning books in the street is far easier than selling them
- And burning flags is more satisfying (and slightly less pongy) than burning incense
- Cat Stevens has had more hit records than George Harrison, proving the power of his faith (that or his record label)

## JACK THE RIPPER – Some Politically Correct names for him

- Jack the Differently Pleasured
- Jack the Person with Special Needs
- Jack the Socially Misaligned
- Jack the Anatomical Investigation Operative
- Jack the Epidermoid Removal Technician
- Jack the Body Remodelling Artist
- Jack the Person of Modified Sanity

## JACK THE RIPPER – Why he might have been known as 'Saucy Jack'

- He would pinch prostitutes' bottoms when they weren't looking
- He stuck his tongue out at the police
- He told that joke about the short-sighted nun and the marrow
- He answered his mother back
- He liked Branston pickle a lot
- He used to fold balloons into suggestive shapes
- He was once suspected of being a *saucière* in a swanky Whitechapel bistro

## JAPAN – 5 words or phrases they find it very easy to say

- Tora! Tora! Tora!
- Banzai!
- Eat lead, imperial Yankee demon!
- Long live the Emperor!
- Take that, Blitish lound-eyed devil!

## JAPAN – One word they find it extremely difficult to say

- Sorry

## JAPANESE CARS – Politically Incorrect names for new models

- The Enola Gay Sedan
- The Oppenheimer 2-litre Estate
- The Jap's Eye 1300 Convertible
- The Death Railway Coupé GLX
- The Pearl Harbor Executive Saloon
- The Nagasaki 1600 DeLuxe
- The Yellow Peril 1500 GTI
- The Dead Dolphin 2-litre Hatchback
- The Kamikaze Supra
- The Hari Kiri 2000 16-valve
- The Protectionist Trade Policy GL

## JESUS – 7 cast-iron reasons why he wasn't the Son of God

- Mary never slept with God and in 4 BC, according to scientists, IVF hadn't even been discovered
- On his birth certificate, under 'Father's Name', it does not say 'King of the Universe'
- At Jesus's school, God never once made an appearance at parents' evening
- Or in the fathers' race at his sports day

- Historical records show that Jesus never sent a Father's Day card to anyone called 'God'
- At school Jesus never once boasted, 'My father created the universe. Yours didn't!' (and then stuck his tongue out)
- All fathers want to protect their children but Jesus was left to die on the Cross

## JESUS – Absolute proof that he was a heroin junkie

- He had long hair
- He was unshaven
- He didn't have a job
- He had strange visions
- He experienced temporary feelings of euphoria
- He disappeared for three days over Easter (to try and kick the habit)
- His body displayed puncture marks

## JESUS – What would happen if he was born today

- The CSA would be on God's back for maintenance

## JOKES – Punchlines to Politically Incorrect masterpieces

- Winnie Mandela!
- Fred Astaire's willy
- 'Big Mac and fries, please'
- 'Peter . . . I can see your house from here . . .'
- Because it would look stupid with four inches
- Attach Velcro to the ceiling
- The coming of the Lord
- The defendant
- To stop them opening corner shops
- A conga line in an old people's home
- Because air's free . . .
- The St Patrick's Day Parade

## KOREAN DELICACIES – The top 10

- Alsatian Spare Ribs
- Sweet and Sour Yorkie
- Great Dane Saté
- Crispy Fried Boxer
- Sausage Dog Chop Suey
- Minced Corgi and Cashew Nuts
- Basset Chow Mein
- Bulldog Spring Rolls
- Shar-Pei with Crispy Noodles
- Stir Fry Pug

## THE KU KLUX KLAN – Why it's much better than the cub scouts

- It does more for your ego being known as 'Grand Dragon of the Realm' than it does being called 'Akela'
- It's more exciting going door-to-door lynching people than it is doing 'Bob-a-Job'
- When it comes to clothing, wearing a flowing white robe and hood is far more mysterious than short trousers and a woggle

- You never need to help old ladies across the road
- Knowing how to make a fiery cross is more impressive than knowing how to make a fire
- There's none of that old bollocks about 'thinking of others before yourself' or 'doing a good turn every day'
- There's nothing like constructing a hangman's noose for teaching you about tying knots
- Instead of going on church parade you get to burn the fucker down
- You're much more patriotic towards the flag (well, at least the Confederate one)
- Obesity, a low IQ and being the offspring of two cousins do not harm your chances of progressing within the organisation

## MARTIN LUTHER KING – Why he wasn't quite as profound as we think he was

- His famous phrase 'Free at last! Free at last!' occurred to him after an unfortunate accident with his zip and his foreskin
- 'I had a dream,' he declared – not telling the assembled masses that what he'd really had a dream about was Sophia Loren and Kim Novak naked in a bath full of tapioca
- The phrase 'That's your lot; anyone who wants a shag, see me afterwards' was cut from his speech at the last moment

## THE LAND – Why we can't go back to it

- Sony have built a factory on it
- Barratt's have built a starter home village on it
- It's heaving with agro-chemicals
- There's a mean-looking BSE-infested bull in the field giving you the evil eye
- We'd have to cross a busy six-lane sub-orbital ring road to get there (and then find it's buried under a feeder road for the ring road anyway)
- British Coal are open-cast mining it
- Some councillor turned a blind eye to Green Belt rules and allowed it to be built on, for £500 and a holiday in Tenerife
- The police would mistake us for travellers and beat us unconscious
- By law, it now belongs to someone with two surnames and four chins

## LANGUAGE – The only two reasons why you might bother to learn a foreign language

- You might want to swear at a foreigner
- You might want to complain about their toilets

## LAPDANCING – 10 reasons why it's better to be a lapdancer than a ballerina

- A ballerina doesn't often get the chance to express herself by gyrating her groin two inches in front of someone's face at the Royal Court
- If a ballerina breaks her leg her career's probably ruined; the only thing to stop a lapdancer is a sex change
- Or suddenly gaining 112 lb
- Or a penis
- A ballerina is surrounded by a whole troupe of camp choreographers and male dancers so the chances of getting off after a performance are zero
- A ballerina needs 45 minutes of warm-up exercises before performing; the only preparation a lapdancer needs is a vinegar douche and a sprinkling of talcum powder five minutes before showtime
- Top ballerinas earn about £250 a week if they're lucky; a lapdancer can have that stuffed down her knicks in used fivers in just one night
- Ballet requires considerable skill and training while lapdancing just requires firm tits and freedom from BO
- If you're a ballerina you have to learn how to perform a *fouette*, an *entrechat* and a *rivoltade*. A lapdancer just has to master doing the splits on a bar counter without falling off
- Ballet is only appreciated by 1% of the whole population; lapdancing appeals to 100% of heterosexual men

## LARD ARSES – 8 excuses fat people always use to try to justify their weight

- 'It's my metabolism'
- 'It's a glandular problem'
- 'It's hereditary'

- 'I'm just big-boned'
- 'I retain a lot of fluid'
- 'The doctor says I'm the right weight for my height'
- 'It's not fat, it's muscle'
- 'My husband/wife likes me this way'

## LARD ARSES – The REAL reasons why they're such fat bastards

- A level of greed that would have made Robert Maxwell look positively benevolent
- A kamikaze attitude towards cholesterol poisoning
- Lack of self-control
- Lack of self-esteem
- Gluttony as a way of life
- Pavarotti as a role model
- An illogical desire to be the butt of people's jokes
- Every Tuesday, Tesco's has a sale of out-of-date cakes
- Jaffa cakes taste *so* good

## LEAD POISONING – Why it's good for today's kids (and society)

- Kids will become too thick to work out how to break into cars
- It will give teachers a great excuse for failing at their jobs
- Gary Glitter can make another comeback
- To ensure the Conservative Party a healthy future
- Mike Reid can revive *Runaround*
- The Body Shop is becoming far too popular amongst the young, threatening our entire system of business ethics
- Lots of kids are vegetarians now – and are not getting their regular dose of brain damage through infected sheep and cows

- The *Sun* newspaper is a national institution and it would be a shame if it couldn't increase its circulation over the next decade
- If all children are thick, there will be an end to school bullying
- Only bright children wear glasses, so increased brain damage will save the NHS millions in spectacles every year

## THE LEAGUE OF NATIONS – Why it didn't work

- Not all countries played soccer as a national sport
- Britain was extremely miffed to be relegated to the second division
- Patriotic British fans disrupted away matches and very nearly started a war with the Swiss
- European colonial powers invaded Africa in the hope of finding some good new players
- Local derbies like England vs France could result in terrible animosity
- Germany visited Poland for an away match – and stayed
- Someone suddenly realised that the League of Nations wasn't meant to be a soccer event at all, and everything ended in confusion
- It spawned that spectacular success we know today as the United Nations

## LENIENT SENTENCES – Why judges hand them out

- They fancy the accused
- They don't fancy the victim
- They don't fancy Michael Howard
- The coin came down heads
- They've met the pertest young boy just the night before and they feel sixteen again
- They thought they were dealing with a parking offence instead of double murder and they're too embarrassed to admit their mistake

- They want to get their own back after the *Sun* criticised their last lenient sentence
- The Lord Chief Justice dared them to
- They'd like to impose a heavier sentence, but they know it would only be overturned on appeal anyway
- The Preparation H has finally worked
- They've eaten too much British beef

## LEONARDO DA VINCI – Why he was a stupid git

- He named himself after a Ninja Mutant Turtle
- He wrote backwards
- He drew flying machines but wasn't clever enough to include a facility for in-flight movies
- The 'tank' he designed didn't even have tracks – let alone a bloody big gun
- It didn't occur to him to paint the *Mona Lisa* nude and spreadeagled
- When he sketched *Madonna and Child* he completely forgot to include her basque with pointed bosoms
- He filled loads of notebooks with drawings of hydraulics when he could have been out on the piazza sketching chesty Italian babes
- He used to drag dead bodies back to his studio to draw, never once thinking that the law might find this suspicious . . .
- He sold the *Mona Lisa* for 20 lira (the price of a new HB pencil and a Cornetto)

## LESBIANISM – Why it's OK with us

- Women are tasty, men aren't
- In hot lesbo movies, there's a distinct lack of hairy bottoms (usually)
- Women with pierced eyebrows are, generally speaking, better off with each other
- It keeps the British dildo industry buoyant
- And unisex barbers

- k d lang makes some good records
- Just thinking about it gives the day a lift

## LIBERALS – Things they say

- It said in the *Guardian* . . .
- Try not to do it again, Slasher
- Of course, Michael Ignatieff would disagree with you there . . .
- Next time, do you think you might possibly not relieve yourself up against my car – if it's all right with you?
- Hello, my name's Melvyn Bragg . . .
- Gosh, yes, darling, of course we don't mind if you marry a 70-year-old syph-ridden Mongolian shepherd. I'll learn a traditional chant for the wedding
- Let him out; he's served three days of his ten-year sentence . . .
- Hello, son, would you like to borrow my heroin needle to shoot up with . . .?
- Islam has so much to offer the West . . .

## LIBERALS – Things they don't say

- Eat lead death, you Argie bastards!
- My face leaves at five; be on it!
- Just wait till I get you home!
- Hang the bastard!
- That is a prime piece of crumpet!
- Have you got the new Steven Segal video?
- What'chu lookin' at?
- Sting, you're a tosser!
- John Woo has so much to offer the West . . .

## LIBERALS – Good jobs for them

- Teacher
- Social worker
- Prison reformer

- Myra Hindley's bottom-wiper
- University lecturer
- Magistrate
- Conscientious objector
- Citizens Advice Bureau worker
- Probation officer

## LIBERALS – Bad jobs for them

- SAS man
- Police officer
- The man who presses the button in the abattoir which operates the steel brain-bolt
- Heavyweight boxer
- Sniper
- Hit-man
- Full back for Millwall FC
- Mafia don
- Bullfighter
- Repo man
- Bailiff
- Hangman

## LIBERALS – Things they're good at

- Getting it wrong
- Getting it completely wrong
- Turning the other cheek
- Turning the other other cheek
- Turning the other other other cheek
- Turning the other other other other cheek

## LIBRARIES – How we could make them more attractive for kids

- Throw out all the books
- Get some video machines in
- Replace the librarians with actors dressed up as Power Rangers

- Replace the signs saying 'No talking, please' with signs saying 'Bad trip cool out zone'
- Put up a skateboarding ramp so that they can skateboard along the study tables
- Or replace the study tables with pool tables
- Scrap readings by local authors and book Pulp or Supergrass
- Take down the posters for the local operatic society and put up posters of Manchester United or Louise
- Take out the study area altogether and replace it with a fast-food franchise
- Take down the sign saying 'Library' and rename the place 'The Maxx Zone'

## LIGHTBULB JOKES – A few of the more Politically Incorrect

Q: How many feminists does it take to change a lightbulb?
A: That's not funny!

Q: How many straight San Franciscans does it take to change a lightbulb?
A: Both of them

Q: How many gays does it take to change a lightbulb?
A: Two. One to change it and the other to say 'Fabulous!'

Q: How many sexists does it take to change a lightbulb?
A: None. Let the bitch cook in the dark!

Q: How many feminists does it take to change a lightbulb?
A: Two. One to change it and one to write about how it feels

Q: How many lesbians does it take to change a lightbulb?
A: Three. One to screw it in and two to talk about how much better it is than with a man

Q: How many Irishmen does it take to change a lightbulb?
A: Eight. One to hold the bulb and seven to rotate the ladder

Q: How many dumb Irishmen does it take to change a lightbulb?
A: One hundred and twenty. One to hold the bulb and 119 to rotate the house

Q: How many feminists does it take to change a lightbulb?
A: Ten. One to change it and nine to form a support group

Q: How many priests does it take to screw in a lightbulb?
A: None. Priests don't screw

Q: How many women with PMS does it take to change a lightbulb?
A: Three – AND DON'T ASK! IT JUST DOES, OK?!

Q: How many anti-abortionists does it take to change a lightbulb?
A: Seven. Two to screw in the bulb and the other five to protest that it was lit the moment they began screwing

Q: How many necrophiliacs does it take to change a lightbulb?
A: None. They all prefer dead bulbs

Q: How many feminists does it take to change a lightbulb?
A: Who cares as long as one of them sucks my dick?

Q: How many homophobic men does it take to change a lightbulb?
A: Two. One to change it and one to get the rubber gloves just in case some gay guy touched the bulb before him

Q: How many Chernobyl workers does it take to change a lightbulb?
A: None, because people who glow in the dark don't need bulbs

Q: How many Iraqis does it take to change a lightbulb?
A: None. Since the Gulf War they haven't had electricity

Q: How many ethnic minorities does it take to change a lightbulb?
A: None – but 200 will march on the power company and demand that it hires some ethnic minorities to do it

Q: How many Germans does it take to change a lightbulb?
A: Two hundred thousand and one. One to give the order that the bulb should be changed and 200,000 to carry it out without question

Q: How many anti-abortionists does it take to change a lightbulb?
A: Twelve. Six to block the entrance to the room, five to hold up pictures of burnt-out bulbs and one to try and convince the person with the new bulb to let the room stay dark

Q: How many lesbians does it take to change a lightbulb?
A: Two. One to change it and one to make a video documentary about it

Q: How many perverts does it take to change a lightbulb?
A: PANT . . . PANT . . . One, but guess . . . GASP . . . PANT . . . GASP . . . what he's . . . PANT . . . GASP . . . wearing . . . GASP . . . GASP . . . when he does it . . . AHHHHHHHHHHHH . . .

Q: How many feminists does it take to change a lightbulb?
A: Fifty. One to change it and 49 to complain how oppressed the socket is

Q: How many Ku Klux Klan members does it take to change a lightbulb?
A: None. They prefer to stand solemnly around and watch the old bulb burn

## LOCAL COUNCILLORS – Things they all have in common

- Strong connections with the building trade
- A predilection for 'funny' handshakes
- Corpulent physiques
- Faces that would stop a clock
- A desire to visit their 'twin town' at taxpayers' expense six times a year
- No interest whatsoever in what you think

## THE LOCH NESS MONSTER – Some simple and rational explanations

- The Scots are mental
- The Scots are pissed
- The Scots are a bunch of lying gits
- The Scots need tourists
- The Scots aren't bright enough to tell the difference between an otter and a dinosaur
- The Scots are laughing at us Sassenachs
- The Scots need their eyes examined
- The Scots need their heads examined

## LONELY HEARTS – Some much more appropriate names for this column

- Losers Column
- Uglies Corner
- Hopeless Pariahs Page

- Inadequates Small Ads
- Desperates on Parade
- The Gullibility Zone
- Defectives Calling
- Social Lepers Classifieds
- Spotlight on Bloody Liars

## THE LOTTERY – 8 Politically Incorrect things to do if you win the jackpot

- Set fire to your brand-new Ferrari Testarossa outside the nearest welfare office, and toast marshmallows in the blaze. Tell anyone who asks what you're doing that you suddenly felt peckish . . .
- Send out your cronies to buy up every toilet roll in a 300-mile radius
- Buy millions of copies of 'Sugar Sugar' by the Archies so that it soars to number one and every radio station feels obliged to play it regularly. Keep on buying it in sufficient quantities to keep it at number one for ever . . .
- Buy up every theatre in the world . . . and stage *Seven Brides for Seven Brothers* in every single one
- Offer someone £50,000 cash . . . if they'll punch their girlfriend in the face
- Open a luxury TV, video and audio superstore in Toxteth. Put no locks, shutters or bars on the place. Keep the shop entirely empty of stock . . .
- Buy one of the only six Bugatti Royale's ever built . . . and then enter it for the demolition derby
- Buy up priceless art treasures and hold an underwater art exhibition. (You won't notice the difference with most Modernists)

## THE LOTTERY – Why it's better to put a pound on the Lottery rather than in a charity tin

- You might win something

- You are helping to keep opera alive
- That millennium party in the year 2000 is really going to be something. The drinks kitty must be huuuuge by now . . .
- If you don't, you just know this is the week your regular numbers are going to come up
- The taxman's slice helps keep our taxes down
- You'll give the charity a tenner – if you win
- It's not your fault there are so many stray cats in the world
- You haven't got muscular dystrophy
- The machine was right next to the fags . . .


## LOVE, ALL YOU NEED IS – 9 things John Lennon needed more at the time

- A bath
- A shave
- A haircut
- A detox clinic
- A new pair of granny glasses so that he could see what he was getting married to
- A good slap around the head for being so naïve
- Someone to tell him that 'I Am the Walrus' was bollocks
- 24 hours without the use of a major hallucinogen
- Paul McCartney


## LUST – Why it's far better than love

- 'Lust at first sight' is considerably more common than 'love at first sight'
- Lust only lasts ten minutes (or five if you've been drinking); love affairs drag on forever
- Love gives you fluttering little butterflies in the stomach; lust gives you a stonking hard-on of cosmic proportions
- It's hard to consummate love against a wall in a back alley

142

- You can lust after Pamela Anderson safely but God help you if you're in love with her . . .
- When you're in love your heart skips a beat; with lust you nearly bust your zip
- When you're in love with a girl you buy her flowers; when you lust after her you buy her a peephole bra and shackles
- Too many people have died of a broken heart
- No one ever died of a broken cock

## MAD COW DISEASE – Some more Politically Correct (and less frightening) names

- Psychologically Different Farmyard Friends
- Dippy Daisy Dilemma
- Wacky Angus Follies
- Zany Clarabell Syndrome
- Eccentric Ermintrude Malaise
- Under the Weather Moo-Moos
- Funny Heffer Complaint
- Capricious Calf Malady
- Foolish Cattle Complaint
- Off-Form Friesians
- Jippy Jerseys
- Barking Bovine Bacteria
- Something that Only Cows Ever Get Disease. Honest. Honest.
- Cow Care in the Community

## MAD COW DISEASE – Other animal diseases they haven't admitted to yet

- Screwy Sheep Scrapie
- Potty Pig Schizophrenia

- Daft Duck Brain Meltdown
- Round the Twist Rabbit
- Stupid Stoat Complaint
- Halfwit Hamster Cerebral Holocaust
- Loony Llama Brain Death
- Spazbrain Snake
- Sandwich Short of a Picnic Parakeet Disorder

## MALE – Why it's good to be a white Anglo-Saxon male

- It's highly unlikely you'll end up with a naff name like Errol
- Or Betty, for that matter
- It's far easier to get into the England cricket team
- And on the board of directors
- The police leave you alone
- And so do desperate drunken men at chucking-out time
- You don't have to eat foul West Indian vegetables
- Or have one tiny pot of fromage frais for lunch
- Old ladies don't cross the streets to avoid you
- And desperate surly men don't cross the street to follow you

## MAN – Why it's much better to be a man than a woman

- You're ten times more likely to get a better-paid job
- And ten times less likely to be sexually harassed
- If you fart or belch in a public place it's seen as a 'good laugh' rather than extremely undignified
- You stand a much better chance of winning a fight
- You suffer no pain whatsoever when your baby's born
- The money you save by not wasting it on tampons can be used for fags and beer
- You're less likely to get ripped off by a builder, plumber or car mechanic
- You don't have to worry about your bikini line

145

- A woman's place is in the home. A man's place is on top of a truly great bird
- You can't get pregnant
- You can sleep with loads of partners and no one calls you a slapper
- You can go into the men's bogs and write puerile graffiti all over the cubicle walls
- While you're there, you rarely have to pay for the privilege of taking a leak
- When you're 50, instead of suffering from the menopause you can be out there, chatting up some young impressionable tart
- You don't have to be arsed with doing your hair and putting on make-up. All you need when you leave the house is a Cloret and a packet of three

## MAN'S WORLD, IT'S A – How you can be sure that this statement is true

- It's well and truly fucked up

## MARRIAGE – More appealing prospects

- Shutting your privates in the fridge door
- Shutting your privates in the car door
- Shutting your privates in any other kind of door
- Watching every single *Play Your Cards Right* ever made
- Having 'Wanker' tattooed indelibly on your forehead
- Stopping a runaway train using just your scrotum
- Having plastic surgery to make you look like Sir Leon Brittan
- Giving up lager for Babycham
- Having your erectile muscles surgically removed
- Selling your soul to Jeremy Beadle
- Wearing women's clothing every day for the rest of your life
- Wearing underpants woven entirely from barbed wire
- Having sex with a porcupine

- Becoming a gynaecologist for bag ladies
- Getting a job as chief taster at the local sperm bank
- Being circumcised with a cheese grater
- Being circumcised with a cheese grater without anaesthetic
- Spending twenty years sharing a prison cell with 'Burly Bates, the Bedfordshire Bung-Hole Buggerer'
- Having a brain transplant with a Woolworths shop assistant
- Having a head transplant with Mollie Sugden
- Buying a Nissan Micra

## MARRIAGE – Why it's a genuinely bad idea

- Would you like to eat beans on toast forever and ever?

## MASSAGE – Forms of massage that don't work

- Bioenergetics
- Acupressure
- Shiatsu/zone therapy
- Osteopathy
- Hot oil massage
- Being pummelled by a burly Japanese masseuse

## MASSAGE – Forms of massage that *do* work

- Swedish
- Unhurried massage in own home by a professional lady
- Topless
- Hand massage
- Being walked up and down on by a Filipino girl in sharp white stilettos

## MASTURBATION – A manifesto; how tossism must be confronted and persecution ended in this country

- Tosser is a tossist word and should be scrapped

- Wanker should no longer be considered an insult, but a term to be worn with pride
- The term jerk should also no longer be an insult
- Jerk-off Pride marches should be organised
- Trendy discos should hold special 'Spank the Monkey' nights (preferably Stringfellows, because their clientele most fit the pattern)
- Masturbators should come together to express their solidarity
- Practising masturbators should come 'out' from under the bedclothes
- Masturbationary practitioners should be given a free hand to express themselves without judgement
- Masturbators should have freedom to congregate – if they really have to
- Masturbators should be allowed to marry – themselves
- 'Jack the Biscuit' must be decriminalised
- Masturbators should be free to join the armed forces and the priesthood
- Masturbators should be better catered for on the nation's television – *Baywatch* and *The New Adventures of Black Beauty* are not enough
- Kleenex should be provided by local authorities free of charge
- Ambidexters will be welcomed into the movement too . . .
- Cabinet members who do not 'out' themselves should be outed by their mums or members of their old scout troop

## MATHEMATICS – Why learning it at school is a complete waste of time

- No one ever got rich by being able to work out the lowest common denominator (except maybe Henry Ford, Lew Grade and Alan Sugar)
- Girls are rarely impressed by a working knowledge of matrices

- Knowing that 23 in binary is 10111 won't help you in a pub fight (in fact, it might even start one . . .)
- Being able to work out logarithms won't help you fix your car by the side of the road
- Vectors are no use whatsoever in hanging wallpaper
- Whatever people may tell you, you don't need to understand quadratic equations to sign on the dole
- Although it might seem like it, long division does not help in doing the football pools

## MEAT – Why it's a million times better than fruit

- It just wouldn't be the same tucking into a roast pawpaw for Sunday lunch
- Or a large stuffed yam on Christmas Day
- 'Pruneloaf' is a stupid name for the singer of 'Bat out of Hell'
- If you put pears and nectarines on a barbecue your guests would probably punch you and then go home
- A nice juicy grape will not fill you up
- Neither will a succulent casseroled mango
- Fruit doesn't bleed when you bite into it
- There's no such thing as the Mediterranean meat fly
- You don't get pips in a lamb cutlet
- And you don't have to peel a pork sausage
- Strawberry tikka marsala would find very few takers
- You can't use the skin of bananas for covering sofas (well, you can, but it would smell and who'd go to World of Bananas for their new suite?)
- Fruit is covered in pesticides and there's no knowing what damage this could do to our bodies

## MÉNAGE À TROIS – Why it sounds good in theory

- If you accidentally call out someone else's name while you're asleep it won't matter – chances are they'll be in bed with you anyway
- It saves lying to your partner about having an affair
- It enables you to write about your experiences to a porno mag – and not have to lie through your teeth
- You can make an easy, direct comparison between both your lovers on the spot
- For once, it won't matter if you don't know which way to turn
- It saves using an electric blanket in winter
- It gives you a chance to practise your French accent when you tell people about it
- If you pass wind rather loudly suspicion will not automatically fall on you
- You can make your friends *really* jealous!
- There'll be two women around to make you breakfast in the morning

## MÉNAGE À TROIS – Why it's bad in practice

- You won't have a clue what you're doing because it'll be like some frantic, naked game of Twister – you'll be lying there going 'Oh yeah! Do it to me, baby!', only to discover it's your *own* hand on your dick
- You're twice as likely to stick your elbow in someone's face
- There are also four elbows that could end up in *your* face (or six if you're still confused about the whereabouts of your own limbs)
- Chances are you'll end up finishing in four and a half seconds, bringing your participation in the event to a rather premature end
- There'll be twice as many women laughing at your pathetic 'performance'
- The third partner might turn out to be a man
- You all end up sleeping in one big wet patch

## FREDDIE MERCURY – Why he was full of shit

- What would he know about 'Fat Bottomed Girls'?
- His slimy songs completely spoiled *Highlander*, which a lot of us paid good money to go and see
- 'Don't stop me now'? Pity they didn't – he might still be alive . . .
- 'Scaramouche, Scaramouche, will you do the fandango?' is hardly profound
- The writer of 'Radio Ga-Ga' should not be treated as a posthumous genius
- A challenge – quote one profound Queen lyric. Go on
- The hamsters tamped it all up the back of his colon

## FREDDIE MERCURY – Why he's not in heaven right now

- He decided it wasn't good enough for him
- He played Sun City
- God can't stand 'Radio Ga Ga'
- He's on a tour of purgatory
- In 'Bohemian Rhapsody' he confessed that he 'once killed a man, put a gun against his head . . .'
- He can't find a banana to pad out his crotch
- Tight spandex upsets the Invisible Host
- With his palate, the Devil wanted him as his personal circumcision machine – and Freddie was only too happy to accept the job . . .
- God doesn't want the choir invisible singing 'Fat Bottomed Girls'
- He just isn't – but all the little hamsters are . . .

## MILLENNIUM CELEBRATIONS – How we'll celebrate the dawning of a brave new century in Britain

- By getting drunk and using abusive language
- By fighting in the streets

- By drink-driving and losing a limb
- In the company of some third-rate Scots git live from Arbroath
- By getting crushed to death in Trafalgar Square
- By staggering home at three in the morning and pissing up the side of a Mondeo . . .
- . . . having just vomited all over the bonnet of a Volvo
- By doing the birdy dance at street parties throughout the land
- By humping some drunk fifteen-year-old in the bedroom under the coats
- In some other disgusting way which thankfully we won't remember come the morning

## MODELS – Why they *should* be skinny

- No one normal could wear those clothes
- 'Waif' looks better in a *Vogue* headline than 'Wobble-bottom'
- Models called 'The Shrimp' or 'Twiggy' sound ten times better than ones nicknamed 'Blobby' or 'La Behemoth'
- Clothes hang much better on someone without tits
- Designers don't have to use several metres of expensive fabric to fashion one miniskirt
- You can get more than two models on the catwalk without any danger of it collapsing
- They're selling a dream, not a reflection
- Lurex looks terrible with clingy sweat stains
- Armani can reintroduce the hoop without any fear of frightening small children and animals
- Cellulite clashes with plaid
- 'Rent-a-Tent' don't have their own designer label
- Designers can imagine they're really pretty young boys in dresses and get all aroused
- *Anyone* can be fat

## THE MONA LISA – Why a dead sheep suspended in formaldehyde is better

- The *Mona Lisa* is élitist, being stuck away behind bullet-proof glass whereas the dead sheep is much more accessible to the public
- You have to go all the way over to France to see the *Mona Lisa*
- If you wanted to (and you might) you could buy the dead sheep exhibit. No money on earth would get you the *Mona Lisa*
- You only have to use your eyes to appreciate the *Mona Lisa*; the dead sheep affects two senses
- You can't make a jumper out of the *Mona Lisa*
- Or have sex with her after the gallery attendants have gone home
- If you were accidentally locked in the gallery overnight you could get to sleep by counting the exhibit
- If you were accidentally locked in the gallery over a long bank holiday weekend you couldn't stay alive by eating – or drinking – the *Mona Lisa*
- It makes grown Welshmen weep
- If someone dies while visiting the museum and needs to be instantly embalmed, they're sorted
- Collies visiting the gallery will find something of interest
- Everyone concurs that the *Mona Lisa* is a fine piece of art by a genius. The dead sheep is far more evocative and controversial
- The *Mona Lisa* was the pinnacle of da Vinci's achievement. Hurst is just beginning to show what he's capable of (a turd suspended in Mazola, anyone?)

## MONEY – Money talks: what is it saying to you?

- Can't catch me!
- Who are you?
- Hello, stranger!

- Long time, no see!
- I'm just passing through on my way to Rupert Murdoch
- So long, sucker!
- Butterfingers!
- Blow me! Blow me!
- Your wife's in love with me, not you!

## MOZART – Why he's no match for Gary Glitter

- Mozart was never known as 'The Leader'
- None of Mozart's concerts relied on gimmicks, like appearing on stage astride a massive motorbike
- Mozart was never backed by 'The Mozart Band'
- Mozart's shoes only had soles half an inch high
- Mozart wore sombre-looking clothes as opposed to a gold lurex suit
- Mozart never sold out six straight nights at Wembley Arena for his Christmas show
- Mozart never had his own fan club
- Gary is a cooler name than Wolfgang. (It's better to be Gazza than Wazza)
- Mozart died young (it's too late for Gary)
- Mozart never won a gold disc for any of his records
- Mozart never appeared on *Top of the Pops* alongside such greats as T Rex, Mud, Sweet and Alvin Stardust
- Mozart didn't write lyrics as good as 'I Love You Love Me Love'
- Mozart was never declared bankrupt
- You can't dance to *Eine Kleine Nachtmusik* like you can to 'Do You Wanna Be in My Gang?'
- Mozart never made one comeback, let alone 48
- Mozart never got his own annual
- Or a free poster in *Look In*
- Mozart never appeared as a guest star on *Shangalang*
- Or knocked Hot Chocolate off the number-one spot
- Mozart was Austrian; Gary is British

**THE NATION OF ISLAM – Why it's a really good organisation to join**

- You get to wear a fez (there's not many right-wing extremist groups that give you the opportunity to do Tommy Cooper impersonations on a daily basis)
- Louis Farrakhan wears a bow-tie so he must be really brainy
- Or a real 'fun guy'
- You might get the chance to meet more fun guys like Colonel Gaddafi
- The guards are all great dancers (they must be, or why else would they dress like MC Hammer?)
- You have the opportunity to be creative and rewrite history
- You hate Malcolm X so you don't have to watch that dreary film by Spike Lee
- You can pick up a great car stereo from the Nation of Islam's bring-and-buy sale
- There're not many better opportunities to network than on a 'Million Man March'
- If you're black, it's very difficult to find any other Nazi party willing to accept you

- You can appreciate the irony of blacks professing faith to an Arabic religion that created slavery

## NATIONALISATION – Other things the Tories could sell off

- Their bottoms
- Sir Norman Tebbit (for glue)
- David Mellor (for pork chops)
- Scotland (for the golf courses)
- Sir Leon Brittan (for live sex acts with something large and spiky)
- Wales (if anyone would buy it)

## NATIONS – 13 nations with really stupid names

- Zanzibar
- Turkey
- Upper Volta
- Chad
- The Congo
- Chile
- Finland
- Andorra
- Dahomey
- Laos
- Mali
- Western Samoa
- The United Kingdom

## NATIVE AMERICAN INDIANS – Some traditional names it's time to bring back

- Redskins
- Injuns
- Pesky varmints
- Renegades
- Savages
- Red devils
- Wig-Wam heads
- Totem Pole toerags
- No-good, two-timin', yellow-bellied skunks

## NATIVE AMERICANS – More reasons why they don't deserve much respect

- Their houses consisted of a bit of rag draped over three beanpoles
- They slaughtered herds of bison – one of the world's most endangered species

- They were the only warrior race that wore moccasins
- Since when was scalping or staking out in the hot sun allowed under the Geneva Convention?
- They encouraged smoking
- They looked like Adam Ant
- They perpetuated sexual stereotypes by only permitting the men to go hunting
- Their clothing was made exclusively from animal skins
- In no way was whooping ever considered dignified for a warrior race
- They considered the tomahawk to be the ultimate weapon
- They were celebrated in a song by the Osmond Brothers
- They had stupid haircuts (especially the Mohicans)
- They wore make-up
- They said silly things like 'heap big wampum' so no one could take them seriously
- They worshipped the buffalo – which is ugly and smelly

## NATIVE AMERICANS – Names they'd rather forget about

- Incontinent Rat
- Cowardly Jackal
- Lazy Sloth
- Arthritic Coyote
- Vomiting Wolf
- Prancing Cow
- Timid Skunk
- Festering Porcupine
- Running Sore
- Verminous Pustule

## NAZI SECRET WEAPONS – 5 ideologically unsound and completely useless V-weapons of World War II

- The V-3; remote-controlled pilotless drone aircraft that dropped toasted marshmallows on to enemy troop formations

- The V-4; a 250mm self-propelled gun that fired a one-ton high-explosive shell with a range of two and a half metres . . .
- The V-5; midget submarine designed to carry 24 torpedoes, able to stay submerged for four days with a range of 3,000 miles, crewed entirely by white mice
- The V-6; an atomic-powered aircraft carrier designed to accommodate 95 fixed-wing aircraft – cunningly disguised as an atomic-powered aircraft carrier designed to accommodate 95 fixed-wing aircraft
- The V-7; a rocket-assisted pig, called Fritz

## NAZISM – Why there's a resurgence in Germany at present

- Because the Krauts are a bunch of fucking tossers

## NEUTERING PETS – DIY methods that are cheaper than going to a vet

- Staple gun
- Soldering iron
- Black & Decker strimmer
- Size 10 DM
- Industrial bolt cutters
- Length of barbed wire and some pliers
- Work-bench vice
- Circular saw
- Piece of string attached to a door handle
- Electric fan without the guard
- A piece of wood with a rusty nail in one end
- Your granny's false teeth

## NEW AGE IDEAS – The truth

- Palmistry – Crap
- Vegetarians – Pooftas
- Tarot – Bollocks

- New Age music – Toss
- Astrology – Shite
- Aromatherapy – Complete wank
- Graphologists – Utter toerags
- Dowsers – Lying gits
- Dowsing – Gobshite
- Psychometry – Wank
- Reincarnation – Never!
- Astral projection – Oh yeah . . .
- The third eye – Complete arse
- The power of crystals – Fuck off!
- Alternative medicine – Do me a favour!
- Shamanic drumming – Pur-lease!

## FLORENCE NIGHTINGALE – Why she was bad news

- She disobeyed her parents who forbade her to become a nurse
- The sight of a woman in a nurse's uniform was enough to cause many casualties to have a relapse
- She worked for very little money, therefore setting a precedent for today's nurses
- She also worked very long hours, therefore setting another precedent
- Many of her patients recovered sufficiently to go back to the Crimean War – where they died horribly
- Her lamp disturbed many patients who were trying to get to sleep

## NOAH – What he should have taken on his ark instead of 'animals two by two'

- Bisexual triplets with the bodies of centrefolds and no morals
- A huge vat of strawberry jelly
- A more modest tub of Vaseline
- A video camera
- A water bed
- A heart-shaped hot tub

- 90 family-size boxes of Kleenex
- Enough Durex Featherlites to hump his way into the record books
- Heart pills
- Willy splints
- Nob cream
- A big sign that said 'Do Not Disturb for 40 days'

## THE NORTH SEA – 12 environmentally unsound tourist attractions

- The Great Turd Barrier Reef
- The Underwater Condom Gardens of Cromer
- The Sewage Discharge Fountain of Sheringham
- The local shit surfing scene
- The Dead Seabird Dump, Felixstowe
- Watching the effluent come in by moonlight
- A unique form of sea spray that's 95% untreated piss
- The Hunstanton Toxic Chemical Aquadrome
- The Dead Fish Aquarium, Yarmouth
- The wreck of the *Exxon Valdez II*
- The wreck of the *Exxon Valdez III*
- The wreck of the *Exxon Valdez V* (the *Exxon Valdez IV* broke up and sank without trace)

## NORTHERNERS – Reasons to hate them

- They come from the North
- You have to keep saying 'What?' when they speak to you
- They have a fascination with smelly, filthy pigeons (probably some form of identification)
- Bernard Manning comes from the North
- They think cloth caps and sensible sleeveless cardigans are high fashion
- They come down to London, take our jobs and sit around in pubs complaining that 'back home' a pint of stout only costs three farthings
- They thought Gracie Fields was good – and still do

- They send all their unwanted children down to London
- They cost us a fortune in dole money
- They think going on holiday to Skegness (or Skeggy, as they affectionately dub it) is a big deal
- It has been scientifically proven that you should hate them (it was in *Omni* or somewhere)

## NUCLEAR TESTING – Why France is justified in carrying it out in the South Pacific

- It would be pretty damned irresponsible to carry it out in the middle of Paris
- Or Cannes
- If they did it in their Antarctic territories it would be catastrophic for the penguin population
- Not to mention that it would probably melt the polar ice cap
- It's *their* bomb
- If you've got it, flaunt it
- They might want to discover the long-term effects of radiation on coral reefs or giant turtles; what better place to conduct their experiments?
- No one tells America not to carry out nuclear testing
- And Australians don't count

## NURSERY RHYMES – Some examples made even more Politically Incorrect than ever before

Old King Cole was a merry old soul
And a merry old soul was he
'Cos he had a dick
That was three inches thick
And it hung down to his knee

Oh, do you know the muffin man
The muffin man, the muffin man,
Oh, do you know the muffin man
Who's gone down on your wife?

Little Boy Blue
Who's got the horn
For the sheep in the meadow
And the cow in the corn
Where is that boy who's in love with the goats?
He's down in the old barn, getting his oats

Three blind mice! Three blind mice!
See how they come! See how they come!
They're tossing off, all day and all night
They wank with their left paw; they wank with their
    right
And that is how they all lost their sight
Those three blind mice

Georgie Porgie, pudding and pie
Humped the girls and made them cry
When the boys came out to view
Georgie Porgie humped them too
(He was a bisexual, that's why)

Rub-a-dub-dub
Three men in a tub
And who do you think they be?
A dancer, hairdresser,
Sociology professor
Shirtlifters, all the three

Bobby Shaftoe's gone to sea
He said he didn't fancy me
He'll be screwed on hands and knees
Now he's in the Navy
Bobby Shaftoe has turned queer
He's nothing but a ginger beer
He's bringing up the Admiral's rear
Now he's in the Navy

Oh dear, what can the matter be?
I've got my bell-end stuck in my zip, you see
Now I can't even go for a bloody pee
I wish I'd been circumcised

Hush little baby, don't say a word
Papa's gonna buy you a mocking bird
If that mocking bird won't sing
Papa's gonna take it right back to the pet shop and ask
for his fucking money back, all right?!

### O.J. – O.J. Simpson's top 13 tips for wife-beating

- Don't knock seven shades of shit out of your woman. Go for eight. Always strive to be the best at what you do
- Don't whup your wife in front of guests – it's bad manners
- Don't be calling her a bitch and threatening to whup her candy ass when the police despatcher is taping the phone call
- Don't go breaking your wife's fingers – how's she supposed to fix your dinner?
- Don't you go breaking her teeth; a toothless bitch is an ugly bitch
- Don't go breaking her legs neither; supposin' you want a beer fetched from the fridge . . .
- Don't hit your wife with your golf clubs. It can affect their swing
- Be sure that the bitch don't have no safety deposit box with her ugly face in it
- Don't be kicking your wife when she's pregnant. Treatment for premature babies costs a shitload of dollars!
- Dead women tell no tales

- Wear gloves
- Don't drop them
- Be rich enough to afford good lawyers

## OAPS – Why they should all be locked up in a home, out of sight and out of mind

- We'd never have to watch Bruce Forsyth again
- Stories about El Alamein and D-Day are boring
- Post offices wouldn't smell nearly so much of piss on pension days
- There'd be less of a queue in Oxfam shops
- They have an unpleasant tendency to sing 'We'll Meet Again' at the drop of a hat
- Their scraggy pet cats wouldn't pooh on our hydrangeas
- We'd have more chance of scoring some stale bread and cakes at Wenzels at the end of the day
- Help the Aged wouldn't keep sending us heartbreaking sob stories every Christmas
- They wouldn't be around to remind us about where we're all heading . . .

## OFFICE SKILLS – Good office skills to employ female workers for

- Seductive cross-referencing of files
- Erotic completion of forms in triplicate
- Alluring 'Whoops, I've lost my furry gonk and it's rolled under my desk'
- Suggestive coffee-making
- Provocative photocopying
- Smouldering typing
- Tempting adjusting of the swivel chair
- Naughty routine dictation
- Sensual shredding
- Sultry hole-punching
- Sexually aware borrowing of pencils
- Hot 'n' ready for it collating of documents

## OLD PEOPLE – Some unkind ways to refer to the 'temporally challenged'

- Wrinklies
- Crinklies
- Crumblies
- Duffers
- Parasites
- Mouldies
- Crumplies
- Grumpies
- Grumblies
- Mugger Bait
- Zimmer Merchants
- The Sholley Brigade
- Feeblies
- Varicosed Vermin
- Brittlies
- Old Age Pricks

## OLYMPICS – 10 events the working class would excel at

- The 100m Velour Shell Suit Hurdles
- The County Court Judgement Marathon
- The Noisy Party Decathlon
- Freestyle Tattooing
- Sovereign Ring Dressage
- 3,000m Shouting
- Featherweight Birdie Dance
- 4 x 100m Shoplifting in Woolworths
- Dangerous Dogs Pentathlon
- Cockney Knees-Up Floor Exercises

## OLYMPICS – New women's sports we'd really like to see introduced in time for the year 2000

- The 1,500 metres splits
- Wet T-shirt relay
- Amateur foxy-boxing
- The long jump (over a pit of fresh warm custard)
- 60 metres breaststroke (with little pigeon feathers)
- The 'tight running shorts run about for a bit' race
- Nude gymnastics (with a special minicam on the parallel bars)
- Pro-am mud wrestling
- The 'no bra' jog

## OPEN-CAST MINING – 10 ways to turn an eyesore into a tourist attraction

- The Gravel Pit Experience
- Slate Park (it's a 'hole' lot of fun!)
- Quarry World of Adventure
- Slurryland – Home of the world's biggest mudslides!
- Stratum! – See the history of the world laid bare!
- The Shale Centre
- The Mini-Grand Canyon Experience
- The Excavation Sensation! (can you dig it!)
- The Gravel-X Rad-Maxx Bungee Zone
- Pet Rock City

## OPERA – Why it's Politically Incorrect

- It discriminates against the aurally disadvantaged
- And the unwaged
- And those who can't understand Italian
- There are very few opera singers of Afro-Caribbean descent
- And no opera companies in oppressive South American countries
- Tenors eat a disproportionate amount of the world's food resources in order to sustain themselves
- Many young male singers were forced to undergo castration as a 'career move'
- Verdi perpetuated the stereotype of circumferentially enhanced people in his 1893 opera *Falstaff*
- Gilbert and Sullivan's *The Mikado* made it acceptable for Westerners to parade as Orientals for cheap entertainment, while giving persons of Asiatic descent joke names like 'Yum-Yum', 'Pooh Bah' and 'Nanki-Poo'
- It's offensive to homosexuals (e.g. Purcell's *The Fairy Queen*, W.S. Gilbert's *Fallen Fairies* and Wagner's *The Fairies* and *The Ring*)

## OPPORTUNITY – 13 possible reasons why it doesn't knock any more in Britain

- It got mugged
- Or stabbed
- It trod in some dog shit in the street and has gone home to clean its shoes
- It's stuck on a sixteen-mile tail-back on the M25
- It's in hospital after eating some dodgy beef
- It couldn't get there because of a rail strike
- It slapped a threatening teenager and is currently in custody
- It's raining (again)
- EU regulations don't allow it
- It's depressed over its negative equity
- It got laid off and is signing on
- People are frightened to open their doors
- It's worried that no one would recognise it

## ORIGINS – Why it's obvious that gays are born, and not made

- There's no kitemark on their bottoms
- Or bar codes
- There's no VAT on gays
- You can't get slight seconds from a gay discount warehouse
- You can't buy cheap gays from Taiwan
- Or counterfeit ones from car boot sales
- Andy and Vince from Erasure would never have passed BS 5750 quality controls
- They don't come complete with an owner's manual with handy connection and trouble-shooting tips
- If you're not happy with yours, you can't send it back
- You never hear of enthusiasts making their own gays in garden sheds

- If one breaks down you can't mend it with a spanner and some sticky tape (although it's fun to try)
- You don't find gays featured on *Supermarket Sweep*

## ORPHANS – Some good ways to taunt them

- Ask them when their school's parents' evening is
- Tell a kid that her parents are actually still alive, it's just that they put her in the orphanage because she was so ugly
- Tell a kid that his parents are actually still alive, it's just that they didn't give a toss about him
- Ask them if they're going to buy a Mother's Day card?
- Ask them how many birthday presents they got from Mummy and Daddy
- Put a white sheet over your head and pretend to be the ghost of their dead parents
- Tell them that Santa Claus only visits children who have been good to their mummy and daddy – and if they don't have any mummy or daddy they won't get any presents
- Tell them that the Devil was their father and a bitch in season their mother
- Tell them that the reason they don't have any parents is because they were created by a mad scientist who put 250,000 volts through a dog turd

## OUTED! – 11 great men of history who thought they were really 'women trapped in a man's body'

- Julius 'Julie' Caesar
- Abraham 'Betty' Lincoln
- Martin Luther 'Natasha' King
- Alexander 'Debbie' the Great
- H.G. 'Henrietta Gertrude' Wells
- Glenn 'Glenda' Miller

- Kaiser Wilhelm 'Tracy' 1st
- Genghis 'Sheila' Khan
- Kubla 'Kathy' Khan
- Shaka 'Carlotta' Zulu
- Moses/Wendy

## OUTED! – 10 great women of history who thought they were really 'men trapped in a woman's body'

- Marie 'Englebert' Curie
- Emily 'Bruce' Brontë
- Nell 'Neil' Gwynne
- Queen Cleopatra (Gazza) of Egypt
- Amelia 'Malcolm' Earhart
- Joan (Barry) of Arc
- Marie 'Timothy' Antoinette
- Queen Boadicea/Norman
- George 'George' Eliot
- Mrs Thatcher

## OUTSIZE CLOTHING SHOPS – Some Politically Incorrect (but far more apt) names

- Mr Fat Bastard
- Arbuckles
- Guts R Us
- Obese About Town
- Tent City
- Maxwells
- Now That's What I Call Humungous
- The Blubber Warehouse
- Bunter's Bargain Clothing
- Monsieur Cochon de Savile Row
- Podge Zone
- Monsieur Blimp
- Tubby Mart
- The Wobble Trading Company
- Bulk Buy
- Ms Zeppelin

- Chunkies of Paris
- The Stout Store


**OVERWEIGHT WOMEN – Why you shouldn't dream of marrying one**

- When you want a shag you have to ask for directions
- When she sits on your face you can't hear the stereo
- Mind you, unless you want to live the rest of your life in a neck brace it's a stupid idea to let her sit on your face
- A three-in-a-bed sex romp is definitely out of the question
- During sex you'll rock yourself to sleep before you can finish
- She'll prefer to stuff her mouth with chocolates rather than anything else
- You'll have to keep turning the lights on to reassure yourself that you're not shagging the duvet by mistake
- If she asks you to drink champagne from her shoe it'll cost a fortune
- If you're fat and she's fat, it's impossible to get your genitals together
- She keeps insisting on showing you her latest Budgie the Helicopter book


**OVERWEIGHT WOMEN – Why you *might* want to marry one**

- If you're that way inclined then you can easily put on her underwear when she's out
- You don't get put off when she's pregnant because you can't tell
- If your secret sexual fantasy is shagging the arse off the Michelin Man – you're set for life!

- You don't need to buy a water bed because her flesh has this wonderful, natural rippling motion
- If she's forgotten to take the Pill you can always use the satellite dish as a diaphragm. Or the dustbin lid
- Every time you have a shag you'll feel the Earth move (it has to, according to Newton's Third Law of Mass in Motion)
- She'll never put on weight – there just isn't any more she can add!
- She'll never know you have a small one – because she can't see over her stomach

## OXFAM – Irrefutable proof that the clothes and bric-a-brac donated to them by the West have ruined traditional African culture

- Masai warriors now wear brown polyester pinstripe suits and tank tops
- The once-proud Zulu now pursue gazelles on semi-inflated Space Hoppers
- The top five names for Botswanan children are now Les, Alan, Derek, Stuart and Woody
- Namibian elders use a Fab 208 annual as their holy book
- Burundi musicians are struggling to get to grips with a Stylophone (and wonder who Rolf Harris is)
- Instead of carving mahogany figurines, the Dogon tribe now express themselves with an Etch-a-Sketch
- Sudanese farmers now decide when to harvest their crops by consulting the magic fibre-optic table lamp
- Chad shamen throw Esso World Cup coins to predict the future. (Nobby Stiles is a particularly bad omen)
- The most sought after item among Kalahari bushmen is no longer food or shelter, but card

number seven (Blériot) for their PG Tips 'History of
Aviation' collection

- Ethiopian priests offer sacrifices to a fold-out poster
  of Little Jimmy Osmond
- Swaziland chieftains resolve inter-tribal disputes
  by playing Ker-Plunk and Mouse Trap
- Somalian merchants barter kipper ties for grain

## OXFAM – Why you shouldn't ever shop at Oxfam

- They never have your size
- Kipper ties will never, ever be 'in' again
- You already have all the James Herriot books
- (And your copies don't have pressed bogies in
  them)
- The old bat behind the counter is willing you to
  say, 'Keep the change'
- Our Price has a far better selection of records
  (unless you're really into Showaddywaddy)
- They don't take Visa
- They don't offer interest-free credit on their
  extensive range of 'luxury' Nigerian raffia fruit
  bowls
- They won't deliver – and you have to carry that big
  painting of 'Clown Crying' all around the high
  street with you
- No one's ever bought a complete jigsaw yet
- No one needs a manual typewriter the size of a
  bread bin with no J or Y keys
- Passers-by think you're poor and needy

## OXYMORONS – Some of the most moronic

- Compassion in Farming
- Concerned huntsmen
- Papal infallibility
- Religious tolerance
- Benevolent dictators
- Open government
- Lengthy prison sentences

- Devoted husbands
- Honourable Members
- Responsible multinationals
- Great Britain
- Mankind
- United Kingdom
- United Nations
- British worker
- Liberal sensibilities
- Moral majority
- Doctor of Ethics
- European Union
- Friendly fire
- Guild of Master Craftsmen
- Ministerial responsibility
- Gracious Majesty
- Proletarian art form
- Open prisons
- Bright future
- *Sun* readers

## OZZY OSBOURNE – Why he's better than k d lang

- All he needs before he goes on stage is one pack of cigarettes – not five packs of HP11 batteries
- Ozzy gets more screaming chicks at his concert than k d lang (just)
- The sound engineer doesn't have to interrupt the recording of his new album because he keeps hearing strange buzzing noises
- If you hang around backstage after an Ozzy gig you'll probably bump into Alice Cooper or Aerosmith – not five assorted women tennis players you've never heard of
- Ozzy's groupies wear skin-tight spandex. kd's groupies wear baggy dungarees
- k d lang has never bitten the head off a bat (in public, anyway)

## PAGE THREE GIRLS – Why they'd make great women priests

- You'd go every Sunday, wouldn't you . . .?
- They know the seven deadly sins off by heart – and can personally demonstrate at least four of them
- They'd brighten up the parish magazine with saucy pin-ups and near-the-knuckle captions saying things like 'Sexy Suzie, 19, is a vivacious vicar with a truly heavenly body! When she spreads the word, she's sure to attract the attention of lay preachers everywhere!'
- Topless sermons could be just what the Church is looking for
- They'd be great at judging prize marrows . . .
- They could sell kisses to raise money for the organ restoration fund
- Or their old underwear
- Long boring readings from the Scriptures are out – because they can't read
- They could demonstrate the story of the loaves and fishes by taking their tops off. Somehow
- They've got bloody fantastic tits

## PARANOID SCHIZOPHRENICS – Good things to say to them

- No. I didn't say anything
- What was that?!
- Why's that car following us?
- Is there something wrong with your phone? I keep getting this annoying clicking
- Who's that bloke with the binoculars
- There's a camera up there!
- Your mother works for the CIA
- They know
- Someone's been calling but every time I answered, they put the phone down
- Whatever you do, don't move . . .
- Do you know, they've got these satellites up there now that can photograph a car number plate from orbit?
- Shhhhhh! Can you hear that?
- Didn't you receive all those letters I sent you?
- We've decided to put you on the Care in the Community scheme. Out you go!

## PAYMENTS – Good reasons to make payments to the Conservative Party

- You're angry at every single person in Britain
- You want to avoid prosecution
- You'd like to set up a highly dangerous toxic chemical plant in the North-East
- You'd like an MP to call your very own
- You want to become an MP
- You need to circumvent the Monopolies and Mergers Commission
- You'd like to be a 'sir'
- You've been passed over for promotion and you want your company to go out of business
- You'd like to come to this country when Hong Kong goes down the toilet

- So they can keep the top rate of taxes down
- You want to meet the ravishing David Mellor in person

## PAYMENTS – Good reasons to make payments to the Labour Party

- You want the British economy to collapse
- All your money is in foreign shares, so why worry?
- You have an IQ of 70 and you don't believe the hardliners will oust Tony Blair within two weeks of an election victory
- You're a professional career criminal and you'd like to see the maximum sentence for armed robbery reduced to two weeks' supervised custody in Chessington World of Adventures
- You're a left-handed Somali-Irish lesbian disabled gypsy with attention deficit disorder and you want to be made Chancellor of the Exchequer (which you will be)
- Your name's Diana and you want to see those bastard Royals get what's coming to them
- Your name's Fergie and you want to see those bastard Royals get what's coming to them (only you don't have any money to give because you've spent it all on cream buns)
- You want to meet the ravishing Roy Hattersley in person

## PAYMENTS – Good reasons to make payments to the Liberal Democrat Party

- You love throwing money down the drain
- So they won't come around and shoot your dog

## PENSIONS – Why private pension schemes benefit everyone

- They give salesmen the chance of a life away from petty crime

- You get to appear on telly talking about how you were ripped off
- They make crooks rich
- They're so complicated, no one understands what they're letting themselves in for
- High-street banks looking for another way to royally stuff you don't have to look very far
- Bosses can use them to bail out their company if it's in trouble
- Bosses can use them to line their pockets
- The government doesn't have to look after you in your old age
- They enable compulsive gamblers to play with someone else's money
- When you retire, you'll find you can afford to eat cat food *twice* a day!
- When you retire, the government will offset your state pension against it, pound for pound – sucker!

## PENTHOUSE – Why it makes better reading than the Bible

- The steamiest stuff you get in the Bible is people 'knowing' or 'begetting' each other; there's nothing remotely like a 'red-hot four-in-a-bed shag frenzy'
- You can't jerk off while reading the Bible (well, you can, but you need a much more vivid imagination)
- The Bible is not filled with useful adverts for penis enlargers and impotence lotions at the back (well, the St James version certainly isn't)
- Likewise, there are no photos of unattractive, cellulite-ridden readers' wives
- 'It is hard for thee to kick against the pricks' (Acts of the Apostles 9:5) cannot compare with 'Slip me your throbbing love pump' (*Readers' Letters*, vol. 12, no. 5) – although it must be said that 'I am black, but comely, O ye daughters of Jerusalem' (Song of Solomon) does have a little more in common

- Lesbo action does not feature prominently on the cover of the Bible
- None of the women in the Bible, not even Mary, is described as having a '38DD chest and gagging for it'
- Abraham was visited by an angel – pretty tame stuff compared to one lucky correspondent in last month's *Penthouse* who was 'visited by his two 18-year-old nieces just after he'd had his luxury jacuzzi installed'
- Jonah was swallowed by a whale; the same *Penthouse* correspondent was swallowed by each of his nieces in turn
- Moses was told to 'Go down'. You can guess what happened in *Penthouse* . . .
- Joseph had a coat of many colours; 'Delightful Denise' in last month's issue was resplendent in feather boa and crotchless red panties. Which is the more alluring image?
- It's more exciting to read about a blow-job than Job
- The stories in the Bible are so fantastic that they *must* be made up

## PERFORMING ANIMALS – Why we need more of them

- Humans can't balance a beach ball on their noses
- Dancing people are ten a penny; a dancing bear is the source of endless excitement and merriment
- They're a brilliant way for lazy and unimaginative ad men to sell products
- If you asked a plumber to jump out of a pool, pivot twice in the air and then balance a brightly coloured beach ball on his nose – and all for a dead fish – he'd tell you to fuck off
- You might have to drive hundreds of miles to catch the rare sight of an elephant standing up on its back legs
- Since Frank Bruno is so useless, a boxing kangaroo might be our only chance of beating Tyson

- There is nothing funnier than the sight of monkeys dressed up as if they were human
- Unless it's cats in little leather jackets
- If we don't teach a tiger to cha-cha now, we might never get the opportunity

## PETER PAN – Things the boy who never grew up missed out on

- Having his hopes and dreams cruelly shattered one by one by one . . .
- Male-pattern baldness
- Watching the French conduct a series of nuclear tests in Never Never Land
- Tinkerbell getting pregnant – by Captain Hook
- Wendy leaving him for an electrician
- Having to take Nana to the vet
- Michael coming out
- Arthritis
- Prolonged bouts of impotence
- Coming home from work and finding his stereo gone and a turd on his bed
- Having his kids emigrate to New Zealand and losing touch with them
- The man who runs his private pension plan appearing on *Crime Monthly*
- Dialysis
- Being reduced to dog food sandwiches before the next pension day
- Spending the last three months of his life in an oxygen tent frantically buzzing the nurse for a bed pan

## PETS – Products to help you put them to sleep

- Ronco Puppy Drowner
- Kitty-Zap Feline Electric Cat Basket
- Acme Gerbil Guillotine
- 'Make My Day' Moggie Magnum
- Humane Hamster Disposer-cum-Liquidiser

- 'Marie Antoinette' Budgerigar Block
- 'Fish out of Water' Goldfish Slayer
- Size 10 DMs: the Stick Insects' Final Friends
- 'Fatal Attraction' Teflon-Coated Rabbit Exterminator
- Miniature Mouse Microwave

## PETS – Some good theories to disprove

- Tortoises always land on their feet
- Hamsters can breathe underwater
- Parakeets can fly with one wing tied behind their back
- Guinea pigs' fur is flameproof
- Mice can go without food or drink for two weeks
- Cats have nine lives
- Dogs have nine lives
- Goldfish prefer living on dry land
- Rabbits can live on a diet of Ex Lax
- Newts can survive being jumped on

## PIG FIGHTING – Why it will never catch on

- Pigs are not naturally vicious creatures and are more likely to spend eleven rounds sniffing each others' butts than going at each other like demons
- Even names like 'Razor Porky', 'Piggy the Demolisher' and 'Smoking Joe Bacon' cannot make the contenders sound very exciting
- Pigs do not have very sharp teeth or claws, and the damage they can inflict with even the best-aimed snout is minimal
- 'Oink' doesn't sound very fierce at the best of times, and a succession of them is hardly liable to drive the crowd into a frenzy
- No one is going to pay good money to see a fight in which the winner is decided by a nibbled-on ear or an accidentally trodden-on trotter

## THE PILL – One reason why it's *not* better than condoms

- Men can't blame their crap performance in bed on the Pill

## PIN-UPS – Women most male pensioners would love to see naked (but the rest of us would rather go blind than gaze upon)

- The Queen
- The Queen Mum
- Busty Barbara Cartland
- Magnificent Mollie Sugden
- Curvaceous Claire Rayner
- Thrilling Thora Hird
- Buxom Beryl Reid
- Vivacious Vera Lynn
- The mother from *The Golden Girls*
- Marvellous Mother Teresa
- Busty Baroness Thatcher

## THE PINK POUND – 13 things that lesbians will probably not be spending it on

- Electrolysis treatment
- Immac
- Iron Maiden albums
- Make-up
- Condoms
- Fruits other than bananas
- Vegetables other than marrows, cucumbers, carrots and courgettes
- Contributions to the Conservative Party
- Presents for their boyfriends
- Spermicide jelly
- Pin-up posters of Brad Pitt
- This book
- Any of our other books

## THE PINK POUND – Other equally bloody stupid names for currencies

- The Shirtlifting Shekel
- The Mincing Mark
- The Faggot Franc
- The Gay Guilder
- The Camp Kroner
- The Pansy Peso
- The Limp-Wristed Lira
- The Bum Boy Belgian Franc
- The Nancy New Zealand Dollar
- The Homosexual Hao

## PIT BULL TERRIERS – Why they make better pets than Yorkies

- If you entered a Yorkie in a dog fight, you'd lose your shirt (and your dog)
- Strutting down the street with a short haircut, tattooed biceps and a Yorkie makes you look like a nutter
- You don't have to waste your money on stupid tartan doggie coats if you've got a pit bull
- Or a velvet ribbon for its head
- If you set your Yorkie on the bloke who pinched your girlfriend, the biggest injury he'd sustain would be a headache from lots of yapping
- Some Yorkies look kind and gentle but can actually be quite vicious. There's never any mistake with a pit bull
- An animal whose main method of attack is running in circles trying to get his own tail will never be a threat to anyone
- No matter how loudly it yaps, a Yorkie will never be an effective guard dog
- It does more for your street cred to have a 'dangerous dog' than a crappy little dog

- A Yorkie isn't likely to get its owner splashed across the front page of his local paper, making him an instant celebrity
- Dog owners should have an animal that matches their own temperament (and IQ)

## POETRY, MODERN – Why it's rubbish

It

Doesn'
t           scaN
or          Rhym
E
Andthe spacingisgratuitous
(Up so floating many bells down)

## THE POLICE – Proof that they're a bunch of racists

- Not one Rastafarian has ever been appointed Chief Constable
- Or even Superintendent
- They work on Saturdays which is the Jewish Sabbath
- Their policy of shooting armed robbers goes against every principle that the Quakers hold dear
- Not one patrol car has enough headroom to permit wearing a turban in comfort
- Police canteens often sell beef sausages and pies even though they know the cow is a sacred Hindu animal
- Their vans used to be called 'Black Marias' – which gives you some indication of who they thought they were going to arrest . . .
- Ditto Scotland Yard's infamous 'Black Museum'
- They refuse to let officers take time off during a murder enquiry to make a pilgrimage to Mecca
- If they want an officer to go on a dangerous undercover mission to infiltrate a Yardie gang they always choose a black policeman

- Their nickname of 'Pigs' is insulting to Jews
- And Muslims

## POLICE – Why the police should be allowed to beat up suspects in the cells

- They can't run away or hide
- It's more discreet than out on the street
- It provides on-site training for police cadets
- If one defenceless man proves too much, they can always call for reinforcements from the canteen
- Beating someone up in the middle of the high street is best left to plain-clothes officers
- They've got to improve their pathetic clear-up rate somehow
- It's easier and more fun than forging confessions
- They get accused of it whether they do it or not, so why not . . .
- Most scrotes arrested eventually get let off with a slapped wrist – so the only real justice they'll receive is a good kicking in the cells
- It gives police officers vital practice for riot control
- Other jobs have fringe benefits . . .
- Other police forces do it, why shouldn't ours?

## POLITICIANS – Why we need them

- To make the rest of us feel honest and virtuous by comparison
- To make the rest of us look handsome by comparison
- To give Rory Bremner and Jeremy Paxman something to do
- To remind us that they're not all locked up yet
- To teach us that anarchy isn't really so bad after all
- If we didn't have politicians, rent boys might starve

**POOR PEOPLE – Why they don't deserve to live**

- They hardly pay any taxes but they're first in line for state hand-outs
- They wear old, unfashionable clothes
- Their cars are also usually old and therefore more likely to pollute the atmosphere
- They're a burden on the NHS, always suffering from the effects of cold and damp conditions
- They eat really unhealthy foods, setting a bad example to the young
- They don't have private pensions and bum off the state when they retire
- They're the last people to donate to charities – and the first to benefit from them
- They give their kids cheap, crappy presents for their birthdays
- And Christmas
- . . . Because they were the first things they could grab in your living room when they broke in
- They're extremely unsociable and if they *do* go to the pub, they hardly ever buy a round
- They refuse to give their children the benefits and advantages of a private education

**POP RECORDS – Cover versions that would be Politically Incorrect for us to suggest**

- 'Are Friends Electric' by k d lang and Kiki Dee
- 'Show Me the Way to Go Home' by Ray Charles
- 'I'm Forever Blowing Bubbles' by Michael Jackson
- 'Dancing Queen' by Boy George
- 'At the Hop' by Ian Dury
- 'Dancing in the Dark' by Stevie Wonder
- 'Tax Man' by Chuck Berry and Gary Glitter
- 'One in Ten' by Elton John
- '(Remember the Days of the) Old School Yard' by Bill Wyman
- 'Splish Splash' by Dennis Wilson and Brian Jones
- 'Needles and Pins' by Keith Richards

- 'Theme from M\*A\*S\*H' by Joy Division
- 'Pretty Vacant' by Kim Wilde
- 'My Love Is Dangerous' by Freddie Mercury

## POP STARS – Suggested new names for Politically Incorrect artists

- Barry Melanin Impoverished (Barry White)
- Vertically Inconvenienced Richard (Little Richard)
- John Lee Sex Care Provider (John Lee Hooker)
- Cilla Person of Colour (Cilla Black)
- Circumferentially Challenged Domino (Fats Domino)
- Processed Animal Carcasses Loaf (Meatloaf)
- Siblinghood of Person (Brotherhood of Man)
- Person of Size Larry's Band (Fat Larry's Band)
- Marvin Alternatively Sexually Orientated (Marvin Gaye)
- Dimensionally Enhanced Country (Big Country)
- Visually Inconvenienced Lemon Pie (Blind Lemon Pie)
- Metabolically Different or Existentially Favoured (Dead or Alive)
- Sun Person Lace (Black Lace)
- Differently Sized Checker (Chubby Checker)
- Cosmetically Different Kid Joe (Ugly Kid Joe)
- Person of Modified Height Jimmy Osmond (Little Jimmy Osmond)
- Nourishment Impoverished Lizzy (Thin Lizzy)
- The Grateful Terminally Inconvenienced (The Grateful Dead)
- Uniquely Extended John Hair Disadvantaged-ly (Long John Baldry)
- Vertically Unconventional Eva (Little Eva)
- Dave Dee, Person of Modified Dormancy, Nasally Enhanced, Celtic Victim of British Oppression and Person of Restricted Stature (Dave Dee, Dozy, Beaky, Mick and Titch)

187

**THE POPE – 12 things we bet he's never seen**

- A copy of *Shaven Hussies*
- A shaven hussy
- A vibrating bed
- A packet of three
- Lapdancing
- Bon Jovi, live
- A monster truck
- The inside of a Wimpy
- His nob, next to a ruler
- The lighter side of abortion
- The other person's view
- Reason

**THE POPE – Why he's a fanny magnet**

- He lives in a palace
- He's so important that he's protected by hundreds of armed guards
- He's head of a huge multinational organisation
- He wears exclusive hand-made clothes
- He's always jetting off around the world
- He hob-nobs with world leaders
- He's really, really, really famous
- He's often on TV
- People worship him
- He has sexy blue Paul Newman-esque come-to-bed eyes
- He promises to take you to Heaven – and he's probably the only man who can make good on that . . .
- He's got a great car (if you think the Popemobile is great, that is)
- He's got a ten-inch whanger (why do you think he wears those loose-fitting robes?)
- He's a virgin so he won't have gonorrhoea

## POPES – 10 Politically Incorrect things for them to say

- So, do you fancy a quick shag, then?
- It's all bullshit – and I'm infallible, so I should know
- I want to be called Desiree from now on
- Fuck all you poor people – we in the Church are doing pretty bloody good
- Cardinal, how could you make that poor girl pregnant? Didn't you wear a johnnie?
- If you don't have my new phone connected by two o'clock, I'm damning you to eternal perdition, *capisce*?
- Fuck off, dickbreath!
- Oy, sinner! Stitch this . . .!
- Get your blessing here, only 700,000 lire! Roll up! Roll up!
- Women can't possibly be priests

## PORNOGRAPHY – Why it's great to be a porno movie star

- You get paid to have sex
- The dialogue isn't too demanding
- You soon overcome your shyness about doing the obligatory clothed scenes
- You can choose a great professional name like 'Dick Strong' or 'Colin Cockhard'
- In any other job, coming early would be seen as a benefit. Here you're rewarded for lateness
- Complete strangers come up to you in the street and say, 'Hey, I'd know that butt anywhere!'
- You can help to feed your expensive drug habit
- You get shafted in other jobs – so what's the difference?

## PORNOGRAPHY – Why we need it

- You try wanking off with a copy of The Yellow Pages – it takes forever

## POSITIVE DISCRIMINATION – 10 nice things to say about the Welsh

- Most of them stay in their own country
- Dylan Thomas and Richard Burton are dead
- Sir Harry Secombe is rather jolly
- Their national emblem is better than the national emblem of Ecuador – or Madagascar
- Sir Anthony Hopkins is quite proficient at remembering his lines
- Caerphilly is a moderately tasty cheese
- Snowdon is OK as small mountains go
- Mary Hopkin was a pretty young thing
- Gareth Hale is reasonably funny
- They love animals

## POTATO FAMINE OF 1846 – Why it wasn't all bad

- It stopped children from stuffing their faces with crisps and ruining their appetites
- It gave many Irish the impetus they needed to visit Boston
- Because one million people died there were more potatoes to go around
- It taught people the importance of not relying on one vegetable
- It forced people into experimenting with lots of new foods
- It was far healthier not eating chips with everything
- Many years later it inspired someone to invent Smash
- It helped the indigenous population to reduce the starch in their diet (drastically)
- It resulted in the unfair Corn Laws being repealed

**PREJUDICES – Fresh sections of society we haven't begun to properly pick on yet, let alone form into 'hate groups' so we can drive around in Transit vans and beat them up at night**

- People with stubby little fingers
- People who walk funny
- The left-handed (a natural target for the Right, one would expect)
- People who look like they don't want a fight
- The bearded
- People whose surnames begin with a 'J'
- People who look 'a bit foreign' after you've had a few pints
- Amputees
- People with sweaty handshakes
- People who drive old cars

**PREMATURE EJACULATION SUFFERERS – Why we should end cruel abuse against them**

- We just should
- Really
- Right now
- Right this minute
- No more jokes about 'going off half cocked'
- Please

**PRISON OVERCROWDING – How we can help reduce it**

- Send convicts to Australia like we used to
- Cut off prisoners' limbs so there's more room in a cell
- Cut off prisoners' heads and keep them cryogenically preserved in hat boxes, 100 to a cell
- 'Accidentally' leave the gate open one night
- Only target criminals nicknamed 'Slim' or 'Lanky'. Avoid anyone called 'Fats' or 'Mr Big'
- Encourage hunger strikes

- Fill the prison library with the complete works of Rosemary Conley
- Put more children behind bars – because they're small
- Put mirrors in all the cells so they look more spacious
- Only put non-serious offenders in jail, because they're not there for as long as serious offenders
- Make everything legal
- Employ even more liberal judges like the ones we've got now
- Put prisoners in temporary accommodation – like Longleat and Whipsnade

## PRISONERS – Why they should all have a colour TV set in their cells

- When it comes to hurling objects at warders, a colour TV set is much more dramatic than a transistor radio
- So they can gradually adjust to shite programmes before being paroled
- It's a healthier way of passing the time than buggering their cellmates
- But if they do prefer to bugger their cellmates, they can turn the volume up so it muffles the screams
- So they can watch *The Bill* and learn that crime doesn't pay (that or get a taste for more action)
- So they can watch *Crimewatch* and catch up with what all their mates are up to
- So they can watch *Crime Monthly* and pick up a few handy hints
- So they can watch *News at Ten* and see themselves earlier on in the day, stripped to the waist, standing on the roof and ripping off the slates
- When it goes wrong it gives them a valid excuse to start a riot

- The adverts are useful for suggesting how they could spend that fifty grand still stashed away after that last bank job
- It's better than having a black-and-white TV set
- So that people who have worked all their lives and can't afford a colour set can get their letters printed in the *Daily Mail*

## PRIVATE MEMBERS' BILLS – Politically Incorrect bills to sponsor in the House of Commons

- Compulsory Crotchless Panties for Female Office Workers bill
- Lowering the Age of Consent to 11 (10 for Pretty Boys) bill
- Big Strapping Black Men Available on the NHS bill
- Disability Benefit for Those Mutilated in Vacuum Cleaner Prank bill
- Provision of Glory Holes in Public Lavatories bill
- No Curtains around Women's Changing Rooms in Department Stores bill
- Full Anonymity for MPs Prosecuted for Exposing Themselves on Hampstead Heath Last Saturday bill
- Subsidising UK Production of Nipple Clamps and Handcuffs bill
- No Criminal Charges Whatsoever for Masturbating over a Photo of Sweep in a Public Place bill
- Making It Illegal for National Newspapers to Print Stories and Photos of an MP in Bed with Those Three Turkish Boys (You Know, the Ones Who Were Wearing My Old School Uniform) bill
- Ending Parliament at Lunchtime on Fridays So We Can Spend More Time with Miss Whiplash bill
- Compulsory De-Clawing of Hamsters, Guinea Pigs and Cavies bill

## PRO-LIFERS – Songs to really wind them up

- 'Bye Bye Baby' – Bay City Rollers
- 'I Got You Babe' – Sonny and Cher
- 'She's Not There' – The Zombies
- 'The Young Ones' – Cliff Richard and the Shadows
- 'Goodbye Girl' – Squeeze
- 'She's Out of My Life' – Michael Jackson
- 'Slip, Slidin' Away' – Paul Simon
- 'She's Gone' – Hall & Oates
- 'Hello Goodbye' – The Beatles
- 'Goodbye Baby and Amen' – Lulu

## PROBLEM FAMILIES – Where we could rehouse them

- The Moon
- In a zoo cage marked 'wankers – do not feed'
- Six feet under
- On the lip of Vesuvius or Popocatepetl
- In a sound-proofed box
- Which is incidentally airtight as well
- Sellafield New Town
- Britain's first underwater city (highly experimental)
- Halfway down a particle accelerator
- Up Jo Brand's arse
- In a vat of concentrated acid
- Next door to the councillors who took five years to respond to other tenants' complaints
- In Hampstead, so that those liberal bastards will get a rude awakening
- Anywhere, so long as it's not next door to us

## PROLETARIAN ART FORMS – True working class art forms

- The tattoo
- The Glasgow kiss
- Wee stains tastefully arranged up your garden wall
- Graffiti saying 'NF We Kill OK'
- Green stuff out of kebabs pavement arranging

- Modern art vomit splashes outside offices
- Carvings on posh cars with house keys
- Chains connecting the ear with the nipple
- Threatening behaviour performance art
- Two-finger mime
- Stone cladding
- *The Shane Ritchie Experience*

## PROSTITUTES – Why it's good to frequent them

- They tell you you're the best, instead of 'a fat useless lump who'll never paint the outside of the house if he lives to be a thousand'
- They don't nag you about watching the football
- They don't want you to put up a shelf for them
- They don't expect a bouquet on the anniversary of the day you first met them
- They don't want you to drive them to B&Q, just round the corner to the nearest alleyway
- They say things like 'Oh, baby . . . oh yeah!!!' rather than 'Have you put the cat out?'
- You try and get your wife to wear a lurex miniskirt and thigh-high leather boots
- They only want some of your pay

## PROSTITUTION – Why it's a great job for women

- You can spend most of your working day in bed
- You get lots of sex
- You don't need any GCSEs
- You don't need experience
- You meet lots of interesting people, like judges and Members of Parliament
- You get paid cash
- Your only outgoing is 50p a week for a postcard in the local newsagent
- You get lots of protein
- You don't have to cook for him or clean his underpants

- How else can you support a £200-per-day heroin habit?
- Men pay to abuse you. Ordinary women have to endure it for free
- It's better to do it for £50 cash than a rancid tandoori and a lousy film
- 'Lady of the night' sounds all moody and mysterious

## PUBLIC TRANSPORT – Why private cars are better

- With public transport, you don't have the sudden thrill of finding a parking space after driving in slow circles for 50 minutes
- You can't get caught dodging your fare in a car
- You can't turn up the radio as loud as you like on a bus
- You can pick your nose in your car and not feel ashamed or embarrassed
- You don't have to give up your car seat to someone who's old, infirm or pregnant
- It's not the same, zooming up a bus lane in a bus
- You don't have the pleasure of knowing that you've beaten the clampers if you travel by train
- You can't cut other drivers up on a bus (unless you're a bus driver)
- You can pretend to stop for a hitchhiker – and then drive off
- You can play 'La Cucaracha' on your horn at 3.30 a.m.
- You can't rev up your engine as people cross a zebra crossing if you travel by train
- You can't slam the doors when you get home at 2 a.m. and wake up the neighbours

## PYROMANIACS – How to get them into more trouble rather than trying to assist them with their problem

- Happy birthday! I hope you like Swan Vestas . . .

- Ring, ring – Hello, is that Richard? I think I've left my cigarette lighter in your flat. It might be in your magazine rack . . .
- Invite them round to watch *Towering Inferno* on your video
- Or *Backdraft*
- Smuggle a Bic to them when you go to visit them in jail . . .
- Slip copies of 'Disco Inferno' or 'Fire' by the Crazy World of Arthur Brown into their record collection, preferably somewhere near the top
- Buy them a flamethrower
- Give them two sticks and a Boy Scout's manual

## THE QUEEN – Why it's better to have a king than a queen

- Queen has a silly double meaning that reduces imperial majesty
- Queens are twice as likely as kings to break wind during solemn events of state
- Kings go off and fight battles, queens just sit around and read soppy potboilers
- Kings age gracefully, queens turn into prunes
- Queens are more often late for the state opening of Parliament because they've lost track of time cleaning behind the cooker
- Instead of affairs of state, queens are much more interested in who Ricky's seeing on *Eastenders*
- Kings hold royal banquets; queens hold Tupperware parties for their ladies-in-waiting
- The King is proud to bear the crown; the Queen only tolerates it because it plays havoc with her hairdo
- If the Queen's suffering from PMS, she might slap the King of Togo.
- Kings wave at the crowds as if they mean it; queens just do it to dry their nail varnish

- In poker, a king beats a queen
- Pretty much the same thing happens in the Saudi royal household

## THE QUEEN'S SPEECH – Why it's indispensable viewing on Christmas Day

- It's a good opportunity for the whole family to go to the toilet before it's time to watch *Raiders of the Lost Ark* (for the fifth time)
- It's inspiring to hear how much the Queen cares for her subjects, however poor or tinted they may be
- It gives us the only proper chance of the year to heckle 'What would you know about that then, Maj?' and 'You don't care! You've got £180 billion in the bank' and flick V-signs at a monarch
- It's good fun to compare the speech to the leaked transcript that appeared in the *Sun* the day before
- It's reassuring to know that the Queen takes such a keen interest in international politics and plays such an active role on the world stage
- It's nice to see her and her children since we hardly get a chance to see or read about them the rest of the year
- You can take bets on how many times she talks about 'peace throughout the Commonwealth' and 'family values'
- It will give us many fond memories when we're a federal state of Europe and she's some rich old bint in an institution somewhere

## QUOTES – Authentic, prime Politically Incorrect quotes for you to memorise – and use

'AIDS can be spread by normal sex between men and women. This is still rare in Scotland'
– *Scottish newspaper*

'You'll all end up with slitty eyes if you stay too long'
– *Prince Philip addressing British tourists in China*

'If you give a woman an inch she'll park a car in it'
– *Chief Constable of Gloucester*

'A woman's preaching is like a dog walking on its hind legs. It is well done, but you are surprised to find it done at all'
– *Samuel Johnson*

'Manchester is not such a nice place'
– *The Queen*

'Every Prime Minister should have a Willie'
– *Baroness Thatcher*

'I would have made a good Pope'
– *Richard Nixon*

'To know the mind of a woman is to end in hating her'
– *D. H. Lawrence*

'Brain work will cause women to go bald'
– *German professor*

'I think I could eat one of Bellamy's veal pies'
– *The last recorded words of Pitt the Younger*

'No man is a match for a woman, except with a poker and a pair of hobnailed boots'
– *George Bernard Shaw*

'Man to command and woman to obey'
– *Tennyson*

'Woman may be said to be an inferior man'
– *Aristotle*

'Do you think the prisoners will regard you as just another screw?'
– *BBC reporter interviewing Britain's first female prison governor*

'Coloured servants out there really don't mind – they get their food and their board, so why should they?'
– *Sir Cliff Richard talking about South Africa*

'Certain women should be struck regularly, like gongs'
– *Noël Coward*

'Wives are young men's mistresses; companions for middle age; and old men's nurses'
– *Francis Bacon*

'There are few more impressive sights in the world than a Scotsman on the make'
– *J. M. Barrie*

'In sorrow thou shalt bring forth children'
– *The Bible*

'He that spareth the rod hateth his son'
– *The Bible*

'All wickedness is but little to the wickedness of a woman'
– *Ecclesiasticus*

'Who's your fat friend?'
– *Beau Brummel, referring to George, Prince of Wales*

'The souls of women are so small
That some believe they've none at all'
– *Samuel Butler*

'I hate a dumpy woman'
– *Byron*

'All tragedies are finished by a death
All comedies are ended by a marriage'
– *Byron*

'She isn't a bad bit of goods, the Queen!'
– *Cervantes*

'He crams with cans of poisoned meat
The subjects of the King,
And when they die by thousands
Why he laughs like anything'
– *G.K. Chesterton – probably predicting CJD*

'I've been rich and I've been poor – and rich is better'
– *Mae West*

'A man is as old as he's feeling
A woman as old as she looks'
– *Mortimer Collins*

'Every woman should marry – and no man'
– *Disraeli*

'Here lies my wife: here let her lie!
Now she's at rest, and so am I'
– *John Dryden*

'As a beauty I'm not a great star
Others are handsomer far
But my face I don't mind it
Because I'm behind it
It's the folks out in front that I jar'
– *Anthony Euwer*

'Guns will make us powerful; butter will only make
us fat'
– *Hermann Goering*

'When I hear anyone talk of Culture, I reach for my
revolver'
– *Hermann Goering*

'Of all the plagues with which the world is cursed
Of every ill, a woman is the worst'
– *Baron Lansdowne*

'What female heart can gold despise?
What cat's averse to fish?'
– *Thomas Gray*

'Man has his will, but woman has her way'
– *Oliver Wendell Holmes*

'I am willing to love all mankind except an American'
– *Samuel Johnson*

'Men are more careful of the breed of their horse and dogs than of their children'
– *William Penn*

'Frailty, thy name is woman!'
– *Shakespeare*

'Many a good hanging prevents a bad marriage'
– *Shakespeare*

'The only good Indian is a dead Indian'
– *General Philip Sheridan*

'What two ideas are more inseparable than Beer and Britannia?'
– *The Reverend Sydney Smith*

## RADON GAS – Suitable names for houses built over sources of this deadly natural gas

- Carcinogenic Cottage
- Dun-Chemotherapy
- Casa del Morte
- Geiger Grange
- Dun-Livin
- Leukaemia Lodge
- The Half-Life Hotel
- Radiation Villa
- Chez Emission
- No. 4 Contamination Crescent
- Bide-A-Toxin

## THE RAF GUINEA PIG CLUB – More Politically Incorrect names for them

- The Burns Brigade
- The Blister Boys
- Pizza Pals
- Cosmetic Cobbers
- Char Chums
- Inflagration Intimates

- Friends of the Fireball
- The Brotherhood of the Melty
- The No-Nose Posse
- Burned Bosom Buddies
- Crispie Cronies
- Geek Patrol
- Roasties
- Toast

## RAMBO – Why he's miles better than Flipper

- John Rambo knows how to use a wide assortment of US and Soviet weaponry; Flipper knows how to balance a brightly coloured beach ball on his snout
- Rambo does it for God and country; Flipper does it for fish
- Flipper 'speaks' in an unintelligible sequence of clicks and whistles; Sylvester Stallone is marginally easier to understand
- Rambo goes wherever the action takes him; Flipper swims around and around a swimming pool
- Rambo blows 'em away; Flipper blows water out of a stupid hole in his head
- Rambo jumps out of helicopters into enemy territory; Flipper jumps out of the water and does a sort of useless somersault
- Rambo looks mean; Flipper has a big goofy grin, and looks like Forrest Gump the day he first discovered his own penis . . .
- Rambo has been trained to deal with every conceivable situation; Flipper has been trained to jump through gaily coloured hoops
- Rambo knows everyone's out to get him; Flipper thinks the world's a nice place . . .
- Flipper gets his own back by splashing people with his tail; Rambo splashes them with a fusillade from his M-16

## RAPE – Judges take heed! These are the minimum adequate sentences we the public demand

- Chemical castration
- Actual castration
- A combination of the two, just to make bloody sure
- Being dressed in a saucy nurse's uniform and flung in a cell with three beefy lifers, one of whom has acquired the nickname 'Spread Them Cheeks Charlie'. This is what is known as doing a long stretch the hard way
- Being smeared with female gorilla essence and then locked in a cage with Kong, the largest (and horniest) silverback gorilla ever kept in captivity
- Having the word RAPIST tattooed across the forehead, preferably with blunt used needles not checked for hepatitis B first
- Being presented with his own severed penis, lovingly preserved in amber
- A good fisting by Frank Bruno (and not in a way covered by the Marquis of Queensberry Rules, being definitely 'below the belt', so to speak)
- Use of a special 'penile guillotine' with a miniature basket to catch the severed head
- Death of a thousand nob-cuts

## REFUGEES – Why it's no fun to go to the pub with one

- They hardly ever have any money for a round
- They bend your ear all evening with their problems
- They're more interested in talking about their five-day walk to freedom through a battle zone than what's happening in the Premier League
- They don't know any good drinking games because alcohol was banned in their country
- They don't speak very good English
- They keep asking you to talk up because their hearing was damaged in a mortar attack

- They mistake the Salvation Army selling the *War Cry* for a secret police raid – and try to glass their way to freedom
- You'll be embarrassed to be seen with them because of the state of their clothes (and fingernails)
- They'll also embarrass you by bursting into tears, thinking of the family they left behind
- Or stuffing a ploughman's in their face in one gulp because they haven't eaten in six days
- Because they haven't had a bath for thirteen days you won't have any luck chatting up women
- They flinch every time the barmaid pulls a pint because they think the pump handle might activate a torture device of some kind
- They don't want to mingle – they just want to sit with their back to the wall, watching the door all night

**RELIGIOUS FILM FESTIVALS – 14 films to make delegates close their eyes and shout 'Woo! Woo! Woo! Woo!'**

- Job: No More Mister Nice Guy!
- Mary Does Nazareth
- Mary Does Bethlehem
- Godzilla vs Jesus
- Dirty Herod
- The Calvary Chainsaw Massacre
- Peter, Disciple with an Uzi!
- The Rocky Horror Resurrection Show
- Corinthians in Space
- Judas Iscariot and the Land that Time Forgot
- Bring Me the Head of John the Baptist
- Dirty Mary, Crazy Joseph
- The Pope Must Die
- The Pope Must Get His Willie Caught in a Blender

## RELIGIOUS INTOLERANCE – Why it's a good thing

- Religious people talk crap
- They're easy to wind up
- Arms manufacturers rely on it to stay solvent
- They're always splitting into factions and killing each other
- Knowing God personally isn't always a fulfilling experience – it can be schizophrenia
- Zealots tell you that every single word of the Bible is true – but Jesus's real name wasn't even Jesus. It was Joshua, but he changed it because 'Josh Christ' didn't quite have the same ring
- They and their inquisitions persecuted us for centuries – it's time the tables were turned
- Ignorance is bliss

## REMEMBRANCE DAY SERVICES – Good things to do during the one-minute silence

- Impersonate a Stuka dive bomber
- Make farty noises with your hand and armpit to the tune of 'Deutschland über Alles'
- Sing 'Why are we waiting? Why-hy are we waiting?' over and over
- Say, 'Look at me, everyone. I'm Douglas Bader!' then do a stupid walk
- Launch into a tirade of abuse about Bomber Harris
- Whistle 'I was Kaiser Bill's Batman'
- Hold a comb to your top lip and goose-step like John Cleese
- Tear the petals off the wreath that's just been laid, saying, 'She loves me; she loves me not', etc., etc.
- Recreate the sounds of the Blitz
- Go for an indiscreet slash round the back of the Cenotaph
- Stick a piece of pizza on your face and pretend to be a representative from the Guinea Pig Club

## REST HOMES – Politically Incorrect pranks to play outside homes for the elderly

- Dress up as the Grim Reaper and impatiently pace up and down outside, looking at your wristwatch
- Lean two or three coffins up against the wall with 'reserved' notices on them
- Play a soundtrack of the Blitz at two in the morning
- Shout 'Mum, I'm here!' and watch a couple of hundred heads all quickly appear at the window
- Shout 'Mum, I've come to take you home!' and see how fast a couple of hundred old biddies can get downstairs
- Dress up as a mad professor and say, 'Eureka! I've discovered the cure for ageing!' and see how fast a couple of hundred old biddies have heart attacks

## RETIRED GERMANS – Things they always claim

- That on 5 August 1940 they were at home with their families, not 1,600 feet over the Kent countryside
- They're Austrian, not German
- They don't know the first thing about operating a Jagdpanzer IV
- That 'Everyone mistakes me for Mengele. How my family kid me about it, ha, ha'
- They wholeheartedly oppose the current wave of fascism sweeping Europe
- They injured their arm in a sporting accident and not during the Warsaw ghetto uprising
- They were in hiding from 1939 to 1945 since they opposed Hitler and everything he stood for
- The scar on their arm came from having a mole removed and was absolutely nothing to do with an SS serial number
- They don't believe in a Fourth Reich

- 'Yes, I was in the Army but only in the catering corps'
- 'That Gestapo uniform hanging in my closet? I hired it for a fancy dress party and completely forgot to return it. Thank you for mentioning it'
- That some of their best friends are Turks
- They were only following orders

## RETIRED NAZIS – What they claim

- I used to be President of Austria
- I used to be head of the United Nations

## REVISIONISM – Why it's really good to rewrite history

- Everyone loves a happy ending

## RIVER POLLUTION – Why it doesn't matter

- We don't live in rivers
- Angling is tedious
- Fish are bastards and deserve all that's coming to them
- It all washes into the sea eventually, anyway
- If you fall in, it's better to dissolve than to drown
- What's an otter or two?
- Only 50% of our drinking water comes from rivers
- We might accidentally create giant mutant swans and then this country could sell the story to Steven Spielberg for millions and millions of pounds

## ROAD RAGE – Why it's understandable

- Suppressing your pent-up frustrations can be dangerous to your mental health
- Getting out of your car and punching someone on the spot is better than following them home and shooting their family

- It's the body's natural defence against high blood pressure
- Drivers who turn left without signalling deserve everything they get
- Drivers who turn left *and* signal still deserve everything they get
- What else is there to do in heavy traffic since Radio 1 FM started playing dance and jungle?
- It's better to take it out on other drivers than it is to do so on your wife and kids
- People who stop for a red traffic light are just asking for a beating
- It makes a good story to tell the other sales reps back at the sad company you work for
- While you're ranting and raving at someone you're taking attention away from the fact that you've got a crappy F-reg Cortina
- While you're pulling someone through an open window you're taking attention away from the fact that you've got a very small penis (and probably a very ugly girfriend)

## ROAD-RAGERS – What triggers them off

- You
- Your car
- Someone else
- Someone else's car
- The fact that you're on the same road
- The fact that you're on the same planet
- Your safe driving
- Sticking to the speed limit
- Indicating
- Using recognised hand signals
- Proper lane discipline
- Going the correct way around a roundabout
- Stopping at traffic lights

# ROCK GROUPS – Some Politically Incorrect names

- Shag Frenzy
- Hymen-A-Go-Go
- Ethnic Cleansing
- Mussolini's Clit
- The Monkey with an Electrode in Its Brain
- The Slappers
- The Saddam Hussein Five
- The Union Carbide Palm Court Orchestra
- The Secret Police
- Dave Dee, Himmler, Bormann, Speer and Hess
- Crack Is Great!

## THE SALVATION ARMY – Why the *War Cry* is a boring newspaper

- There're no juicy front-page headlines like 'Was Jesus a Space Alien' or 'Holy Trinity in Bizarre Love Triangle'
- There's no 'Page 3 Salvation Stunner!'
- Or 'Win £10,000 in Spot the Sinner'
- Or 'Play £1,000 Bible Bingo'
- They don't sponsor the 'William Booth Memorial Wet T-Shirt Contest'
- They don't carry premium phone line adverts at the back such as 'Bang My Tambourine 0898 36725', 'What the Sergeant Saw 0898 32564' or 'Fallen Women 0898 64182'
- It's light on paparazzi shots of starlets with skimpy dresses and huge cleavages
- It might be filled with stories about vicars – but none of them have been caught in bed with two women and a large courgette

## SAS – *The One that Got Away*. Other, less heroic, SAS books

- The One that Shat His Trousers
- The One that Put His Hands Up
- The One that Shot an Unarmed Man
- The One Who Ate a Beefburger and Went 'Bibble-Bubble-Bibble' All Day Long
- The One Who Actually Got an O-Level
- The One with the Funny Stare that No One Wanted to Sit Next to in the Land Rover
- The Ones Who Went Off Together and Committed Unnatural Acts
- The One Who Ran Off when the Shooting Started
- The One Who Didn't Write a Fucking Book Afterwards (Oops!)
- The One Who Pretended to Be in the SAS, So That He Could Write a Bestseller

## SAUDI ARABIA – Five things that King Fahd really hates

- ██████████████
- ██████████ ██████ ███donkey
- ██████ ███████ men
- ████ ██████ ████pert buttocks
- Being called a ████████ual

## SAUDI ARABIA – One thing that King Fahd really likes

- Censorship

## SCHIZOPHRENICS – How to wind them up and convince them their medication isn't working

- Very obviously follow them for a day with a camera and a microphone
- Put a pair of deer antlers on your head and say you're from the CIA
- Dress up as Jesus and tell them they have to paint the M25 blue

- Get a friend to wander past the two of you casually dressed as Santa Claus. Claim that you saw nothing
- Run around screaming, 'The earth is going to explode!'
- Come into the room dressed as a Maori wielding a chainsaw and proceed to sing 'Agadoo'
- Paint yourself green and say you're an ambassador from the planet Mars. Instruct them to clear the way for the landing of the Imperial Martian Fleet by demolishing the nearest police station. Give them a Martian Particle Crusher Device (also known as a sledgehammer)
- Phone them up, say you're Satan and that they must eat their own right foot before midnight or they'll be eternally damned
- Phone them up, say you're Sting and that they must eat their own right foot before midnight or be eternally damned (the effect's the same)

## SCHOOL SPORT – Why it should stay on the curriculum

- It gives jobs to teachers too dumb even to teach technical studies
- It is an ideal torment for fatties
- Communal showers can be very informative
- So many kids go on to a career in professional soccer, it would be a crime not to teach it
- It gives thick-as-pigshit pupils some sense of self-worth
- If you plunge off the wall bars onto your face, you can get time off
- Unpopular kids can be drowned in the swimming pool and the whole thing laughed off as 'youthful high jinks'
- Knowing that you're doing something you really hate and that's a real waste of time helps to prepare you for getting a job

## SCHOOLS – Some 'league tables' that parents ought to demand from schools in their borough

- How many kids have got knifed there
- How many ounces of crack cocaine have been confiscated from pupils
- How many teachers were sacked for touching up pupils
- How many times per minute is the word 'fuck' used in the playground
- How many kids from the school have been convicted for shoplifting during lunchtime
- How many children have had their noses broken for wearing the wrong trainers
- How many first-years have come home in tears over the course of the school year
- What percentage of moronic thugs the school includes in its numbers

## SCHOOLS – Why teachers are so opposed to school tests and league tables

- They're afraid of people finding out the truth
- They reveal how crap most teachers are at their job
- Teachers are scared that their pay will be linked to performance – and that they'll all end up earning £2.30 a year
- League tables reveal which schools you shouldn't send your child to in a million, billion years, threatening them with closure and their staff with getting the sack
- When you read about your child's school's performance, you withdraw them immediately if you care at all about their education, thus plunging school standards even further
- Tests reek of discrimination in favour of the clever – something teachers are 100% opposed to

- League tables reek of discrimination in favour of good schools – something teachers are also 100% opposed to
- They're terrified that tests will lead to streaming – and that someone in the staff room will draw the short straw and end up having to look after a 100% cretin stream, spending the rest of the term trying to teach them their own names
- Streaming helps bright pupils get ahead – and who wants inequality?
- Headmasters are embarrassed when their institutions become headline news as the shittiest school in Great Britain
- They're all middle-class liberal gits, so of course they would be

## SEA POLLUTION – Why it's absolutely brilliant

- All the fish will float to the surface and it'll be easier to catch them
- If our fish are poisoned, the thieving Spanish fishermen will take them back to their home ports and give everyone in Spain the screaming shits
- If we eventually kill off all the fish, the Spanish trawlers can't steal them any more!
- In 20 years' time we'll be able to walk across the Channel – and the Tunnel can bugger off
- In 30 years' time we'll be able to drive across . . .
- If we all stand at Dover and blow in the direction of France, Calais will be assaulted by a stink-wave of incredible proportions
- No more ferries can sink, because they'll just get stuck fast in the gunge
- When we go swimming, we can be 100% sure there are no sharks about
- And no jellyfish, no Portuguese men-of-war, killer whales, Moray eels, sea snakes or starfish

- In 2,000 years' time, scientists will capture our turds floating in the ocean and be able to tell exactly what we ate in the late 20th century

## SECRETARIES – Why they're just like housewives

- They don't need any 'proper' qualifications
- They sit on their butts all day long
- They spend two-thirds of the day gossiping
- They get to make loads of cups of tea
- They get paid very little
- They think they're always busy
- They're always on the phone to their friends
- They complain that no one appreciates what they do
- You sleep with them

## SELLAFIELD – What researchers who work there soon discover

- An extra finger or two on their hands
- An extra finger or two – on their heads
- That most men do not find bald women attractive
- A shadow on their lungs the size of Lake Windermere
- One of their ears in the washroom sink
- That the half-life of plutonium is very, very long
- That the full life of a radiation researcher is very, very short
- A sperm count of minus 20
- That friends stop coming round for dinner parties on the flimsiest of excuses
- They can write up their notes at night by the light of their buttocks
- That you spread Strontium 90 on croissants at your peril
- That their ears take on a life of their own
- That working in the beautiful, tranquil Lake District really isn't worth it

## SENTENCES – Seemingly Politically Correct ones for judges to dole out

- A harsh word or two
- A suspended finger-wagging
- A non-custodial shrug of the judicial shoulders
- Two weeks in the Caribbean, with no hope of remission
- Six months' talking-to, suspended for two years
- A withering scowl
- Life without imprisonment
- Life, commuted to fuck all
- Bound over to do it again

## SERBIA – Why it should be invited to join the European Union now

- It has an awful lot in common with Germany
- We haven't already got a European corpse mountain, so it would be a novelty . . .
- If we need someone to cull British cows, the Serbians could be brought in to rape and machine-gun them for us
- They could assist us in building the future of the European Court of Human Rights

## SHAKESPEARE – Classic works made Politically Incorrect

- The Maiming of the Shrew
- The Battered Wives of Windsor
- The Rape of Lucrece
- Tightarse Andronicus
- King Leer
- The Two Consenting Gentlemen of Verona
- Piss Off Back Where You Come From, Othello
- A Midsummer Night's Wet Dream
- Ham-let

## SHOOT TO KILL – 11 previous policies the British Army was correct to drop

- Shoot to slightly graze
- Shoot to miss completely
- Shoot to hit yourself because you're holding the rifle the wrong way round
- Shoot to tease
- Shoot to tickle
- Shoot to hit an innocent bystander
- Shoot to hit your best mate
- Shoot to Xhuptej (no one could understand it)
- Shoot to bring down that bull elephant (irrelevant to Northern Ireland, not to say politically incorrect)
- Shoot to annoy
- Shit to kill (a typographic error that would have had 80% of the British Army in the long-term care of colon specialists)

## SHOOT TO KILL – One policy the British Army should seriously consider

- Shoot to kill Anthea Turner

## SHOPLIFTING – Why it's recommended in supermarkets

- You never ever need to have a pound coin for the shopping trolley
- You won't get stuck behind some git in the 'Cash Only' line who insists on paying by cheque drawn on some obscure Bank of Hormuz
- Or someone in the '6 Items or Less' line with two trollies overflowing with cat food
- Your weekly shop comes to precisely nothing
- You can spend the money instead on lottery tickets and win the jackpot so you can pay the supermarket back again

- If you're a woman, you can stuff melons under your coat to impress the opposite sex – and provide dessert for four
- If you're a man, you can do the same trick with a cucumber
- The shops condone stealing by making an allowance for this sort of thing called 'shrinkage'
- You won't feel guilty about buying tuna that's not dolphin-friendly – because you didn't technically buy it
- It provides employment for store detectives
- And people who make those security cameras
- It's far safer than ram-raiding

## SHORT MEN – 10 things they can't do

- Go out with 99% of women
- Play basketball
- Reach to put on the kettle
- Go into rough pubs
- Impersonate Dale Winton
- Buy porno books from newsagents without jumping up and down and drawing attention to themselves
- Join the police (even if they wanted to)
- Reach the pedals
- Make a dramatic entrance
- See eye to eye with you

## SHORT MEN – 11 things they can do

- Start wars
- Spot instantly if your flies are undone
- Give you a blow-job standing up
- Head-butt you in the bollocks
- Join a travelling troupe of performing dwarves
- Get into the Odeon at half-price
- Go out with that woman from the Crankies (and feel ten feet tall)
- Stand a good chance of duffing up Don Estelle

- Get a job as Ronnie Corbett's stunt double
- Identify with Bilbo Baggins
- See eye to nipple with you

## SHORT, SHARP SHOCK – What's wrong with it

- 'Short' does not allow for protracted suffering
- 'Sharp' is not nearly as good a word as 'excruciating'
- The 'shock' referred to isn't an electric one

## SINGLE PARENTS – Why it's great to be one

- You don't have to worry about whether your partner will beat you up
- Or leave you
- You zoom up the queue for council housing
- You get to go out with loads of other men
- Or women
- You've always admired how your mum coped with bringing up you, Errol, Prakesh, Mick, Luigi, Mehmet, Jane, Little Bear and Stefan all on her own
- Family outings are that much cheaper
- You can flirt with the teacher at parents' evening without having to be too discreet
- You can flirt with anyone, anywhere without having to be too discreet
- You get to leave work early to pick up your child
- You can read about you, and people like you, in the Tory press every day

## SIT-COMS – Politically Incorrect ones we'd love to see

- Loathe Thy Neighbour
- Steptoe and Gun
- Thick as Welshmen
- Please, Sir, Actually Teach Me Something Today
- Men Behaving Naturally
- For the Love of Rover

- And Mother Makes Five (Not Including the Sheep)
- Never Mind the Quality, Feel the Prick
- Going Straight
- Are You Being Buggered?
- One Foot in the Twat
- Rising Prick
- It Ain't Half Right Wing, Mum
- Adolf and Eva

## SIZE – Why it does matter, no matter what they tell you

- No one ever advertises dildoes the size of gnats' cocks
- No woman ever moans with delight, 'Oh! You're so small . . .!'
- No woman ever says, 'Slip me just a little bit of it . . .'
- No woman ever boasts to her friends that her boyfriend is hung like a squirrel
- There is no market for cosmetic 'penis reduction' surgery
- The chat-up line 'I've got a prick the size of a Twiglet' really doesn't work
- You don't hear women say, 'It was the dinky little bulge in his jeans that got me going'

## SLAVE AUCTIONS – 8 reasons why they were an absolutely terrible idea

- You had to get up really early to attend the viewing
- The catalogues cost a fortune
- The commission the auctioneer took was criminal
- The auction rooms were often crowded and stuffy
- You only had to blow your nose or blink at the wrong time and you'd find yourself lumbered with two strapping six-foot field hands or a family of six cotton pickers that you didn't want

- Wave to an old friend and you'd suddenly find yourself knee-deep in Negroes
- It was hard to concentrate because the lots kept singing 'Swing Low, Sweet Chariot'
- You had to be so careful not to purchase a counterfeit Negro (blacked-up Irishmen looking to advance their social standing)

## SMOKY EXHAUSTS – Why they're useful

- If you're trying to follow someone through busy traffic you can always see where they are
- All the soot protects the exhaust pipe from the build-up of rust and makes it last longer
- It's safer since it makes other drivers keep their distance
- If you're being chased by an assassin on a motorbike you can cause a smokescreen and lose him
- If you've got a severe BO problem the fumes will disguise it
- In case you forget, it's a constant reminder to get your car tuned up
- If you're photographed speeding through a red light the police won't be able to read your number plate
- Once you scrape off enough carbon you could exert enormous pressure on it and turn it into diamonds
- They're much more effective for suicide than clean exhausts

## SOCCER – Why it's better to be a soccer star than to work in a charity shop

- You get paid more
- Charity workers don't get paid a fortune in sponsorship from Nike

- No one ever got a share of a £15 million transfer fee from Scope to the Imperial Cancer Research Fund
- If you cry on the pitch, people think you're passionate. If you cry in the shop, they get embarrassed and leave
- Not one Sue Ryder worker has ever been invited to advertise Walker's crisps for megabucks
- No one plays Fantasy Charity Shop Staff
- You can hang out with the likes of Cantona and Giggs, rather than an old lady with a lazy eye and a white cardy
- The RSPCA thrift shop is seldom if ever televised live on Sky Sports
- You don't have to do anything difficult, like adding up prices
- If you did a big juicy gob in the charity shop, you'd probably be sent home

## SOCIAL SECURITY – Names for this scheme that are far more apt

- Scrounger's fund
- Sponger's money
- Beggar's allowance
- Leech's grant
- Lazy bastard's payment
- Parasite's subsidy
- Pauper's concession
- Work-shy wage
- Freeloader's remuneration

## SOLICITORS – Why they should refuse to handle Legal Aid cases

- They attract the wrong sort of clientele
- They end up spending their time on boring cases about eviction notices and unfair dismissal which are very, very dull

- And very, very, very, very unprofitable
- No one got made a partner by their sterling work for a housing association
- There's far more kudos in winning a celebrity £400,000 in a libel case than in winning some manual worker £400 for losing his hand in an industrial accident
- Legal Aid clients usually respond to defeat in the courts by smacking their lawyer in the mouth
- Every hour they spend working late trying to defend one of the homeless is an hour less they've got to enjoy in their £350,000 house
- There's little to be gained in fiddling time sheets for a client on Legal Aid
- Why should their regular clients who are happy to pay £250 per hour subsidise the riff-raff?
- The sticker they have to put in their office window might leave a dirty mark on the glass

## SOUTH AMERICA – Why the entire region's crap

- It was colonised by the Spanish and Portuguese instead of one of the sensible European powers like Britain
- It's strictly Catholic
- It includes Argentina and Chile in it
- And Peru and Colombia and . . .
- Shooting children is considered part of a policeman's duty
- Torture is considered respectable
- They like to dance the Samba
- And the Lambada
- You can do GCSE Death Squad at school
- Andean pan-pipes sound bloody horrible
- Every leader of every country is called El Presidente, looks greasy, has a military uniform and jackboots, smokes big cigars and has a secret bank account in Switzerland

- Have you seen the stuff they export to Oxfam shops to sell?

## SOUTHEND – 11 things you won't find there

- Anyone whose friend's name isn't, apparently, 'Oy, wanka!'
- Anyone whose child isn't called 'Fuckin' Shut Up, Willyer'
- Five square inches of beach without oil or a dog turd on it
- Five square inches of bare flesh without a tattoo on it
- A pair of tits without a filthy great love-bite on them
- Anyone with an ounce of sense
- A car with a tax disc
- A car without a Simply Red cassette
- The cream of Europe's yachting fraternity
- Anything to do if you don't like bingo, chips or video games
- Skegness

## SOYA – 12 things far tastier

- The combination of nail clippings, pubes and old soap left in the plughole after a bath
- Sump drainage after a 20,000-mile oil change
- The contents of your colon
- Stale dog drool
- Guinness
- Rancid school semolina
- Fifteen-year-old vinegar
- Cough linctus
- Shampoo
- Processed sewage
- Raw sewage
- Gravy made from a combination of Preparation H and iodine

**SPLITTING UP – 11 cruel parting gifts to give to your once loved one**

- A packet of 'Stonk-On Erecto 2000' pills
- A penis enlarger
- A blow-up doll with a photo of your face superimposed over its face
- A book entitled *How to be Good in Bed*
- A book entitled *The Joy of Gay Sex*
- A bar of soap
- A large pack of odour eaters
- The local phone number for the Samaritans
- A rubber face mask
- The address of a good plastic surgeon
- A bottle of Paracetamol

**STALKERS – Why they're not all bad**

- They make you feel wanted

**STEVIE WONDER – 10 jobs it's not advisable for him to do if he ever decides to get out of the music business**

- Knife thrower
- Bomb disposal expert
- Lion tamer
- Commercial airline pilot
- Air traffic controller
- Neurosurgeon
- Chainsaw juggler
- Formula One racing driver
- Golf pro
- Proof reader

**STING – Why he prefers the Amazon to the Tyne**

- It smells better
- It isn't full of Newkie Brown bottles and condoms
- It's easier to understand what the natives are saying

- There's more shipbuilding on the Amazon
- Everything's green. In Newcastle, the only thing green is the puddles of spew you find in the city centre on a Sunday morning
- In the Amazon it only rains 200 days of the year
- The natives think he's a god – rather than a giant wanker who sold out

## STRAIGHT – how the Politically Correct would like to see this 'homophobic' word replaced

- Gayjacket
- Gay line
- Gay ahead
- Gay edge
- Gayforward
- Gayaway
- Gay out
- The Gays of Gibraltar
- The Bering Gays
- The Gays of Hormuz
- Dire Gays

## STRAIGHT – Why it's better to be straight than gay

- You can shag Pamela Anderson rather than the chubby one out of Erasure
- You don't have to pretend to like crappy old Abba records
- Your dad will speak to you
- Your mates will urge you on rather than urge you away
- You don't have to read boring and obscure avante-garde English novels
- You can go on *Blind Date*
- Or *The Shane Ritchie Experience*
- You can let your body go
- You can talk about football properly with your mates, because you're more interested in a player's skills than his tight buns

- You don't get beaten up so much
- You can join the armed forces and indulge in heterosexual activities like shoving broom handles up new recruits' bums
- You can be a Member of Parliament and not have to resign in disgrace just for having sex with your partner
- Michael Barrymore

## STRIP CLUBS – Why more should open

- They provide employment for women
- And the ex-boxers who wouldn't have anything to do unless they stood on the door
- It takes men's minds off their dreary day-to-day existence
- Women have to take their clothes off at some time during the day anyway; this way they get paid for it
- It gives women the chance to juggle their bosoms in opposite directions
- The police know exactly where to go if they want to talk to members of the underworld and other low-life
- It's an opportunity for sad men to meet their own kind
- It's something to do on a wet Tuesday afternoon
- It provides women with a springboard to stardom as international dancers
- Men have to have a wank somewhere . . .
- It keeps perverts off the streets

## STUDENTS – What we're actually paying for when we give them grants

- A chance to avoid facing the real world for three more years
- An opportunity to lose their virginity
- A chance to see the latest indie bands on the circuit

- Organised drinking contests that end in *ad hoc* spewing sessions
- Far too many 2:2s and 3rds
- The money to go down to London to support Feminist Gay Vegetarian Homeless Ethnic Disabled Peruvian Poets on massed marches
- The chance to wear stupid clothes
- An average of 13.34 pints of Snakebite per week of term
- Lessons in advanced – if redundant – Trotskyism, disguised as BA (Hons) Geography
- A qualification that in the end employers tell them means they're too talented to start at the bottom and too inexperienced to start anywhere else

## STUPID – Why it's great to be stupid

- You can amuse yourself for hours trying to peel a Dairylea triangle
- There's always something to watch on telly
- You can eat beefburgers to your heart's content
- You can go out with page three girls and not have them say 'You what?' to every comment you make
- There are lots of opportunities in roofing and felting
- You're never short of like-minded people to talk to
- People don't expect much from you
- You can go to France for £1 with the *Sun*

## SUPERHEROES – Welsh superheroes that never caught on

- Sheepman
- Welsh Rarebit – Commander of 'Fromage Force'
- Choir Boy
- The Human Leek
- Captain Caerphilly
- Jones the Superhero
- Bach-Man and Robin the Boyo Wonder
- Major Miner

- Captain Lllyyyllllggghgllyyflffghl
- Dai Hard
- Justice League of the Rhondda

## THE SWORD – Why it IS mightier than the pen

- A fourteen-carat gold nib is no match for the finest Sheffield steel when it comes to decapitating a marauding Zulu
- Would you choose to fight a duel with a Papermate?
- The Queen would look daft trying to knight someone with a quill
- Errol Flynn wouldn't have been nearly so impressive swinging from a chandelier holding a Bic
- The Scots would lose all credibility if they did the Fountain Pen Dance
- You try running someone through with a biro
- Blackbeard the Pirate would not have struck fear into the hearts of his enemies if he boarded their ships with a Platignum clenched between his teeth
- No circus visitor would pay good money to watch a pen swallower
- When it comes to disembowelling, a Mont Blanc is not the most efficient tool for the job
- If you tried to beat a Sheaffer into a ploughshare it would just snap

## TARZAN – Why the lost 'Lord Greystoke' is actually the perfect working-class role model

- He hangs around with a bunch of apes
- He communicates by grunting
- He likes to go around bare-chested
- He hasn't a clue who his real dad was
- He's not married to Jane, although they live together
- He probably learned his manners from a chimpanzee
- He doesn't have any GCSEs
- He's never even considered a career in banking or the Civil Service
- He carries a knife
- He terrifies the local black population

## TATTOOS – What they say about you

- It's Butlin's again for me next year!
- I like manual labour
- Shakespeare's not my cup of tea
- I went to Calais for a quid with the *Sun*
- 'Eng-er-land! Eng-er-land!'

- I follow Chubby Brown on tour
- That Jim Davidson; what a laugh!
- I used to love this tart called Beryl – and the fucker won't come off now

## TATTOOS, FACIAL – What they say about you

- Look at me and we'll both end up on *Crime Monthly*
- I did it, Judge, and I don't care
- Life on the dole is great!
- Don't let your daughter go out with me
- I've been in care since I was five
- The medication can only do so much
- Have Stanley knife, will travel
- Glue is my drug of choice
- I'm not a vegetarian
- Cousins shouldn't marry
- Come on, Millwall!!!

## TAXES – Good things to tax to make the elderly squeak

- Scraggy old cats
- Being old
- Orthopaedic stockings
- Hairnets
- Sholleys
- Zimmer frames
- False teeth
- Insulting wigs
- Visiting your favourite grandchild
- Weeing the bedsheets
- Using the phrase 'In the good old days' or 'I remember when . . .'
- Elasticated stockings
- Tins of chicken-and-liver Whiskas
- Rheumatoid arthritis
- Having Xmas dinner with their family
- Being born before 1930

- Using the lavvy more than once a day
- Talking crap for hours on end to each other in Tesco's
- Being hard of hearing
- Using a hot-water bottle between the months of August and April
- Calling people 'lovey'
- Saying anything nice about the Royal Family
- Heating and lighting

## THIRD WORLD WORKERS – Why they should quit complaining that US training-shoe manufacturers only pay them 16p an hour

- How much does a six-year-old need, anyway?
- They get paid twice as much as anyone working for 8p an hour
- Or five hundred times as much as people working for 0.03p an hour
- If the US companies paid them £150 an hour they would soon be out of business, and all the workers would be out of a job
- It only takes them four minutes to earn enough to buy a penny chew
- Or 593 hours to afford a pair of the £95 trainers they're making
- A rise of just 4p an hour represents a whopping 25% pay increase; the nurses have to make do with less than 5% and they're much more skilled
- For their wages they have no responsibilities or worries (apart from making sure their fingers and hair don't get caught in fast-moving, unguarded threshing equipment)
- There's plenty of scope for overtime (20-hour days are quite common)
- Even with 25% income tax, they'll only end up paying around £250 a year; Western workers would die to pay that sort of tax

- It helps them understand the Western notion of irony (i.e. the shoes they are manufacturing in cramped, oppressive conditions actually represent personal freedom, fitness and wealth . . .)

## TIPS – Why we shouldn't tip tradesmen

- Have you ever had a *good* haircut?
- If waitresses want more money, they shouldn't do waitressing
- No-one tips you for doing your job
- Taxi drivers are dangerous, miserable, conniving sods – so why tell them to 'keep the change' when 'get some driving and charm lessons' would be a much more appropriate tip
- So a bellboy carries your bags to your room – that's what he's there for, for Christ's sake
- Why tip removal men who have just scraped all the wallpaper off your stairway, sat on your box of fine bone china to eat their sandwiches and farted in every room of your new house?
- Only working-class people get tipped – and they'll only waste it on booze and cigarettes and copies of the *Sunday Sport*
- They're never grateful – they just look at you like you've spat in the palm of their hand or something

## TOILET PAPER – Good things to print on it as a novelty

- The marriage vows
- The Magna Carta
- US Bill of Rights
- The royal crest
- Reproduction of *The Last Supper*
- Gray's 'Elegy in a Country Churchyard'
- Picture of the Queen
- Psalms
- Any of Winston Churchill's speeches
- Any of Winston Churchill's diaries

## TOO RICH OR TOO THIN – 5 other things it's impossible to be

- Too well endowed
- Too frisky
- Too unfaithful
- Too tired for oral sex
- Pamela Anderson's love slave


## TOURETTE'S SYNDROME – Why it's difficult to raise public sympathy for this terrible, debilitating mental affliction

- A television appeal for research funds is out of the question – because the programme would be far too obscene ever to broadcast
- Nobody wants to help someone who's just called them 'shitting-fuck-bollocks'
- Attempts to raise public awareness by having a Tourette's syndrome sufferer appearing regularly on *Blue Peter* were abandoned after just four seconds
- The version of *Jackanory* read by a sufferer led to the end of several previously distinguished careers
- Encounter groups and other attempts to integrate sufferers into the community often end in fist fights
- You daren't go near someone with a collecting tin who's simultaneously verbally and phlegmatically assaulting you
- Tourette's syndrome charity shops are too offensive for many to enter – with their signs saying 'bumhole hats', 'ringpiece ties 30p each' and 'Shit-arse-pooh-pooh books nob, 30p paperbacks, 40p anus hardbacks. Wank'
- It's just too funny to take seriously
- Very few people believe the disease even exists. They think sufferers are just typical 'kids of today' – and they're probably right
- Nobhole

## TRADESMEN – Bad clients for them to rip off

- Anyone in the legal profession
- Anyone who knows someone in the legal profession
- Anyone with more than just a hint of intelligence
- Anyone who has anything whatsoever to do with *Watchdog*
- Another tradesman
- Anyone who knows your home address
- Anyone working for the local Trading Standards Authority, the Health and Safety Executive, the Inland Revenue or Customs and Excise
- The editor of *Which?*
- The chief clerk of the Small Claims Court
- Themselves
- Their mum

## TRADESMEN – Good clients for them to rip off

- The old
- The visually impaired
- The stupid
- The foreign
- The inept
- The stupid, the inept AND the foreign (but how often can you hope to get called out to the White House?)
- Anyone not falling into the above categories but who is nonetheless extremely gullible

## TRAMPS – How to humiliate them

- Offer them 25p to drop their trousers in front of you
- Tell them they may *sniff* your empty can of Special Brew if they sing 'If I Were a Rich Man . . .' for you
- Offer them a packet of fags to walk the length of the street on their hands. As they try, collect all

the loose change that falls out of their pockets and
run off
- Tell them they're now giving free meals to tramps
at Buckingham Palace; just ask a policeman at the
gates
- Offer them a bite of your cheese roll if they dance
the Charleston; in front of you
- Ask them if they'd do anything for money. When
they say yes, tell them to kill themselves for a quid
- Mistake them for Lemmy from Motorhead

## TREE HUGGERS – Threats they respond to

- 'Move, or the elm gets it!'
- 'Take another step and I slap this cheeseplant!'
- 'Back off – I have a trowel and I'm not afraid to use
it!'
- 'I know what you're thinking, punk . . . did he fire
five squirts of DDT or six? Do you feel lucky? Do
ya, punk?'
- 'Runaway bulldozer! Look out!!!'

## TREE HUGGING – 10 pastimes for eco-warriors which are much more fulfilling

- Sapling Fondling
- Bush Groping
- Hardy Perennial Petting
- Plant Frottage
- Thicket Stroking
- Vegetation Fingering
- Shrub Caressing
- Hedge Cuddling
- Undergrowth Rubbing
- Marrow Molesting

## TROUSERS – Why women shouldn't wear them

- You wouldn't get such a good look at their legs

## TURBANS – Much better uses for them than as a silly hat

- Emergency fan belt if your car breaks down
- Emergency tow rope if your car breaks down and there's no way you can fix it
- Replacement roller towel if the one in the pub runs out
- The rope in an impromptu tug-of-war contest
- Flying scarf to perfectly complement a Baron von Richtoften fancy dress outfit
- Toilet paper after you underestimated both the strength of a curry – and the distance to your house
- A sling if you get your arm broken by a mindless gang of racist thugs
- A head bandage if the same gang gives you a good kicking
- Petrol bomb fuses for use by Sikh extremists in Pakistan

## TURKEY – Some reasons why you might possibly choose it as your holiday destination

- You like having your bottom pinched by old men stoned on hashish
- Your idea of a dream holiday is spending at least ten days clinging to the toilet bowl
- The burly, swarthy, sweaty, mustachioed type really gets you going (they're the girls of your dreams)
- Your idea of a holiday romance is having someone ejaculate over the back of your head during a long bus journey
- What your home is really missing is a tatty, smelly, cheapo carpet made by six-year-old child slaves
- You enjoy playing Falafel Roulette
- You are a convicted sex offender searching for your roots

- You have taken a considerable wager on how many flies can possibly settle on a single piece of fruit in an Istanbul market
- You are nasally challenged and long for a truly odour-filled vacation
- You never got around to seeing *Midnight Express*
- The Lebanon was fully booked up
- You hate yourself

## THE TURKISH GOVERNMENT – Things it's far more concerned about than human rights

- Resurfacing the Ankara–Izmir Highway
- Commissioning the 156th series of *Shamir the Sheep Shagger* on Turkish State Television
- The grand opening of the Euphrates Aqua Park & Lido cum Sewage Treatment Plant
- Decriminalising 'interfering with goats' – and indeed, obtaining a European grant for it
- Its forthcoming entry for the Eurovision Song Contest
- Breaking the legendary 1988 record for Turkish Delight production
- Its covert cannabis exports
- Whether they should have changed Constantinople to Istanbul after all
- Trying to sneak into the EU
- Upsetting the Greeks
- Attracting young male tourists with skin like silk and eyes of azure

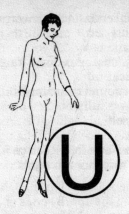

## UNIVERSAL SUFFRAGE – Why it was a huge mistake

- Thick people can vote
- People who don't support your party can vote
- People who believe politicians can vote (if they're let out for the day)
- Women who actually fancy John Major can vote (if they can see their way to the polling booth)
- Things were much quicker at polling stations when only one man could vote in the entire ward
- People with no money can vote for parties who promise to give them some
- Who'd have thought working-class people would vote Tory?

## UNIVERSITY LECTURERS – How to be a Politically Incorrect one

- Give essay grades according to bra cup sizes
- Call all your female students 'dear', 'love', 'honeybunch' or 'cocksucker'
- Teach Ayn Rand instead of Karl Marx
- Display a big portrait of the Queen in your office

- Burst into the Feminist Soc meeting and yell, 'Tits out for the lads!'
- Tell attractive students in your care that their assignment this week is down your trousers and ready to be picked up . . .
- Insist that everyone stands and sings the National Anthem before tutorials
- Say that your office is closed for redecoration and that one-to-one tutorials will be held at the local Forte Post House motel, Room 27
- Insist that all your male students wear suits and ties to lectures – and all your female students sexy French maid's costumes

## THE UNTOUCHABLES – Whom we should extend this venerated Indian tradition to in Britain

- Professional darts players
- Ford Transit drivers
- Families who appear on *Family Fortunes*
- Plumbers
- Local councillors
- Estate agents and their families
- The unemployed
- Page three girls
- Anyone from Essex
- The Welsh. Immediately

## THE V-CHIP – Other censoring TV microchips we'd like to see

- The Shane Ritchie Chip
- The Party Political Broadcast Chip
- The Anything with Penelope Keith in it Chip
- The Oh No, Not the Fucking Two Ronnies Again Chip
- The Embassy World Masters Snooker Championship Chip
- The Programmes with Welsh People in Them Chip
- The Patronising Commercials that Insult Our Intelligence Chip

## VEAL CRATES – 11 adjectives estate agents would use to describe them

- Cosy
- Snug
- Humble
- Bijou
- Starter
- Homely
- Intimate
- Sheltered
- Compact
- Modest
- Unpretentious

## VEAL CRATES – They're not so bad: 10 things that are even smaller

- A starter home from any of the major house builders
- A two-bedroom semi from any of the major house builders
- Your car boot as you load up for the first time to go on a family holiday
- The leg-room in any Multiplex cinema
- Kate Moss's bra
- Any of the supermodels' brains
- The chances of you getting off with a supermodel (especially if you tell them about this bit in the book)
- Your penis, when your girlfriend compares you to her last boyfriend
- The number of people who seriously think that there's nothing wrong with eating beef
- The accommodation for chickens on factory farms

## VEGELAIT – Other traditional British products the EU want to nobble, by giving them new and unappealing names

- Chocolate (Vegelait)
- Liquorice Allsorts (Boiled Cow Yum-Yums)
- Black Pudding (Crusty Blood and Effluvia Munch)
- Pork Sausage (Pig's Cocky and Nipple Slither)
- Pot Noodle (Glutomonosotomatepolyoxideriboflavin Chem-Slush)
- Digestive Biscuits (Fish Oil Crunchettes)
- British Red Wines (Cat's Piss Contrôlée)
- Yorkshire Pudding (Spunky Plop-Plop)
- Tripe (Instant BSE Food)
- Haggis (Ovine Intestinal Wrap)

## VENISON – Why we should all eat more

- Whoever heard of Mad Deer Disease?
- Bambi is *too* cute

## VIDEO NASTIES – 10 reasons why they're good for your kids

- Kids like them
- It keeps them quiet while you're playing with their Sega Megadrive
- While they're hiding behind the sofa whimpering, they're not getting up to any mischief
- They think you're really great for letting them watch them
- You can watch them too
- They give your kids an interest in common with all their mates
- They provide them with an advanced familiarity with human anatomy
- They teach them how to defend themselves with a screwdriver, blow-torch and chainsaw
- They have far more in common with the real world than all that Winnie the Pooh and Budgie the sodding helicopter crap
- When the authorities find out, your kids will get taken into care and you'll be able to get some peace and quiet at last

## VIOLENCE – 10 extra-violent children's TV shows we'd like to see

- Trumpton Reservoir Dogs
- Small Talk Costs Lives with Ronnie Corbett
- Force 10 from Chigley
- The Guns of Pogles Wood
- Where Clangers Dare & Enter the Soup Dragon (double bill)
- Mary, Mungo and the Predator
- Bad Lieutenant Sooty

- Natural Born Woodentops
- Hector's House of Horror
- Aliens IV – Rosie and Jim

## VOTING – Why it's not a *complete* waste of time

- It gets you out of the house
- A gentle walk to the polling station is good for your health
- You might find some money lying on the pavement on the way
- You might meet old friends that you haven't seen in years
- You can practise your cross-making skills
- If you tug on the string real hard, you can score yourself a free pencil from the booth
- You may meet the one true love of your life on your way to or from the polling station
- You can use your voting card to scrape ice off your car windscreen in winter
- You can write a funny message to the person counting the ballots, like 'Help, I have accidentally been locked inside this ballot box' – which is sure to bring a smile to their face . . .
- You can spoil your ballot paper by writing 'They're all wankers' across it in big letters – sure to get a nod of approval from those counting the votes
- You can pass the time of day chatting to canvassers outside the station
- You can combine the trip to the polling station with some shopping or walking the dog
- You can help maintain the illusion that you have a say in anything at all
- You can make deeply hateful and despicable people feel better about themselves by voting for them as if you like them
- Whoever wins and fucks up the country, you can say, 'Don't blame me. I voted for the other lot'

### WAR – Why it's better than peace

- Go to your local video shop; how many peace movies are there?

### THE WELSH – Just one more reason to despise them

- They seem to think that Pot Noodles taste 'gorgeous, man'

### WELSHMEN – Why there are no Welsh characters in *Star Trek* (probably)

- The Vulcans hate them too
- They are not allowed to leave Earth in case they offend other members of the Federation by their mere presence
- All the characters are nice
- The translation devices can't cope with silly accents
- They all failed the Star Fleet entrance exam
- 'Boyo' means 'arseface' in Romulan and nearly led to an interstellar war
- Sheep are extinct in the 24th century

- They all died out in the great 'Sheep Gonorrhoea Terror' of 2075
- Jones the Transporter Chief sounds wrong
- There is no role for a 'First Officer in charge of Leek Growing' on board the *Enterprise*
- Male-voice choirs are superfluous to space exploration
- Mining for Dilithium crystals is done by robots
- They'd make the Klingons look too handsome
- They'd make the Klingon language sound almost sensible
- Wales was closed down in 2010
- Just imagine fellow slaphead Neil Kinnock playing Captain Jean-Luc Picard. No one would take any notice of him (just like when he was head of the Labour Party)

## WESTERN CULTURE – Why it is clearly superior

- Banging two sticks together hardly competes with one of Mendelssohn's great choral pieces
- The Egyptians only built three pyramids – we've built tens of thousands of Barratt homes in a fraction of the time!
- Sticking a bone through your face is hardly the mark of a cultured people
- Who invented rock 'n' roll?
- Africa has never produced an author of the stature of Jeffrey Archer
- As Michael Jackson gets whiter, his music just keeps on getting better and better

## WHEELCHAIRS – Why they shouldn't be allowed to take part in the London Marathon

- It's cheating; everyone else has to run the race the hard way
- They get in the way of the proper runners like the people dressed as gorillas or the panto cow

- Getting to the start-line by public transport is extremely difficult and will probably delay the race for everyone else
- Their wheels might get tangled up in the tape across the finish line, making it unusable for the following year
- They can coast downhill, something that able-bodied runners have yet to master
- If a disabled runner comes first, he or she will find that wheelchair access to the winner's podium is extremely restricted
- The person giving out the medals has to stoop which is bad for their posture
- They might run over the foot of Liz Colgan, ruining her chances of a win for Britain in the Olympics
- Their commitment and perseverance put the rest of us to shame

## WHITE-COLLAR CRIME – Why it's got a lot going for it

- It's unlikely that it'll end in a police shoot-out
- You don't need a look-out and a getaway driver on your payroll
- You need a computer terminal and a password, not a sawn-off shotgun and a stocking mask
- You can do it without even leaving your office
- It doesn't involve leasing the shop next to the bank and digging a bloody big tunnel
- You won't accidentally blow yourself up handling a bought ledger account
- You won't be double-crossed by a gang member called 'Freddy the Ferret'
- The courts will look more favourably on you than someone who shot dead eight people in an off-licence hold-up that went terribly wrong
- At your trial you can say you're senile and get off (P.S. You can keep your fucking Guinness)

250

## WHITE FLIGHT – Why white people are leaving the cities

- They can afford to

## WHITE HETEROSEXUAL MALES – Why it's bloody brilliant to be one

- You get all the good jobs
- You can drive an N-reg BMW without getting stopped every 60 yards
- You can drive a P-reg BMW without getting stopped every 30 yards
- You can drive any car without getting stopped every 30 yards
- People don't go 'heterosexual bashing'
- The worst nicknames you get called are 'Whitey' or 'Straighty'
- You don't get ugly old men undressing you with their eyes
- You don't get pretty young men undressing you with their eyes
- No one prejudges you
- You can identify with 95% of all the leading figures in economics and politics
- You get to make the rules
- You never have to waste time having to prove yourself
- You know that there's a better-than-average chance of you nobbing Pamela Anderson

## WHITE LIBERAL GUILT – 3 reasons not to feel it

- You're black
- You're a fascist
- It's bollocks

## WIFE-BEATING – Bad wives to beat

- Wives who have just taken delivery of a new mail-order ginsu knife collection
- Someone else's wife – like Chris Eubank's, for example
- A wife who's one of TV's Gladiators (and who could crush you like a twig)
- Sara Thornton

## WIFE-BEATING – Good wives to beat

- Small wives
- Frail wives
- Elderly wives
- Wives who have recently had a demanding operation
- Wives with the use of only one arm
- Cornered wives
- Wives who won't go to the police
- Wives who love you too much to leave

## WIVES – 6 good reasons to cheat on your wife

- Brunettes
- Redheads
- Blondes
- Blondes with their roots growing out
- Strange kinky bald birds
- Men dressed up as curiously exotic women who have that little something extra to offer

## WIVES – Things wives just don't understand

- How you can get sexually aroused by the Little Mermaid, Tinkerbell and Pocohontas
- Why socks don't need to be changed every day
- The offside rule
- Casual unimportant remarks like 'I wish you looked like that!'

- How you can love them – and still lust after their best friend
- How you can love them – and still go to bed with their best friend
- The satisfaction that comes from making an Airfix Lysander
- The screen giant that is Steven Segal
- Clothes bought on a credit card are not 'free'

## WOMEN – Why they're the inferior sex

- They're not as strong as men
- They can't fight for toffee
- They look girlie (well, most of them)
- They do all the crap jobs around the house
- They're shorter and have less muscular development
- They have to go to the toilet every 20 minutes
- They think Brad Pitt is a big deal
- They cry at soppy films
- They go off quicker than men
- Name one major battle won by a woman (except for female suffrage, of course)
- They put up with men

## WOMEN – Why they make the best secretaries

- Who wants a man to sit on your knee?
- Or go to a two-day conference to Brighton with you?
- Or wear a tight blouse and even tighter skirt?

## WOMEN – Why they should be made to walk around naked

- They just should
- For some of us, it is our only chance to see a real-life naked lady

**WORKING MOTHERS – Why secretaries who've just had a baby shouldn't be allowed to return to work**

- It's unfair that they should earn child benefit *and* a salary
- Especially after receiving all that maternity pay
- And a leaving present
- They take time off if their baby is ill, disrupting the workplace
- Their baby photos distract all the women
- Their engorged breasts distract all the men
- They can start lactating at any given moment, dripping milk onto a vital report and smudging it
- They prevent school leavers from getting their first job
- Their recent Caesarean means that they can't lift 24 rolls of fax paper or crouch down to clear the jam in the photocopier (and someone else has to stop what they're doing and help them out)

**X-FILES – Politically Incorrect story lines we think the producers should use (just as long as they pay us big bucks first)**

- Deep Throat reveals the true reason why he got his nickname
- Scully is abducted by Greys who make her wear a French maid's outfit in their spaceship and then proceed to conduct scientific experiments like seeing what happens when they spank her with a table tennis bat
- Mulder's sister returns from her abduction with a message from the aliens: 'We must slaughter all the whales if the human race is to survive.' Her advice is taken seriously and the Stealth Blubber Bomber is scrambled
- Area 51 is revealed as the place where nothing is going on. Area 69 is where all the action is
- A strange book suddenly materialises within a top-secret USAF base. It's written entirely in the language of the Navajo Indians and when translated turns out to be *Mein Kampf* (that or the patient notes from Claudia Schiffer's gynaecologist)

- An anonymous figure leaves a video of an alien autopsy outside Mulder's office. When he puts it in the VCR it turns out to be *Debbie Does Dallas* (wide-screen) – which, compared to the autopsy he was expecting, is far more interesting, not to say marginally more arousing
- Scully discovers that her father had been one of the biggest security risks to the US Government. Not only was he involved in a project to create an alien/human hybrid, but secretly he was a professional Debbie Reynolds impersonator
- Mulder discovers that Nazi scientists were secretly flown to the US after the war to work on developing the process of breast augmentation ('Operation Paperclip' was a cover for 'Operation Blub-Blub-Blub-Blub-Blub')
- Mulder and Scully investigate a series of cases involving Spontaneous Human Ejaculation
- The 'Cancer Man' hangs about outside schools, handing out free cigarettes to children

## X-RAYS – Good things for doctors to say to make patients paranoid

- 'I'd say two months. Tops'
- 'Oh dear . . . Oh deary me . . .'
- 'See that shadow on your lung? It's nothing to worry about. Probably a fault in the developing'
- 'Yes. It *starts* as a broken arm'
- 'I can't believe that you're still alive!'
- 'Look! Just stay away from me, OK?'
- 'It's not a doctor you need, it's a priest'

## YORKSHIRE – Some Politically Incorrect things to do during the annual water shortage

- Get a camcorder and make your own version of *Sink The Bismarck* with Airfix models and a paddling pool filled to brimming
- Wash and wax your car every evening just to piss off the neighbours
- Set light to neighbours' houses or scrubland so the fire brigade has to keep putting the fires out
- Install an Olympic-size swimming pool in your back garden. Refill it twice daily to make sure it's hygienic
- Try and turn your front garden into a paddy field
- Make a scale working model of the Niagara Falls from your bedroom window
- Recreate the story of Noah's Ark using just a model ark and a hosepipe
- Turn the whole of your downstairs into one big jacuzzi
- Pretend you're Howard Hughes and have a bath every half an hour
- Turn on the bathroom taps, put the plug in and go out – so you can claim on the insurance for a new hall carpet

- Go up to the local reservoir and piss in it, saying you're doing your bit for the country
- Put notes through all the doors down your street ostensibly from the water board saying that the water in the system has been contaminated and everyone should leave every tap in their house full on for the next ten hours to flush it through

## YORKSHIRE – Things you will find in a Yorkshire reservoir

- Puzzled Yorkshire Water staff scratching their heads
- Bloody big cracks

## YORKSHIRE – Things you won't find in a Yorkshire reservoir

- Water

## YOUNG OFFENDERS – Why it's a pity they hang themselves in prison cells

- It costs the Prison Service a fortune in replacement sheets
- People would pay good money to see them do it in public

## ZOMBIES – Why discrimination against the living dead is wrong

- The word zombie is politically incorrect and should be replaced with the terms 'life-disadvantaged' or 'mortally different'
- People who complain about the stench of rotting flesh are just zombiephobes
- The living-advantaged should be more tolerant of zombie alternative lifestyle practices – such as eating the brains of the living and playing tug-of-war with their intestines
- Zombie children have an equal right to education and should not be segregated just because of their propensity to bite
- The law is blatantly zombie-ist and needs to be changed. Cannibalism and the tearing out of still-beating hearts should be decriminalised immediately
- As zombies cannot have children, they should be allowed to adopt. There is no reason to always assume they will eat the child – just because this is what's invariably happened in the past
- So what if their heads fall off?

# Politically Correct/ Politically Incorrect Dictionary

Thinking of taking up a place at university? Considering applying for that job at Channel 4 – or any of the other jobs advertised in the *Guardian*? Or do you just want to talk crap?

Whatever your motives, here are the key 'Politically Correct' phrases you must learn.

**Access Control Supervisory Technician**
Bouncer
**Acutely optically inconvenienced**
Blind as a bat
**Acutely optically and chemically inconvenienced**
Blind drunk
**Alternatively body imaged**
Lard arse
**Alternatively acquired**
Nicked
**Alternatively living**
Dead
**Alternatively co-ordinated**
Clumsy
**Alternatively co-ordinated and rectally inclined individual**
Clumsy arse
**Alternatively educated**
Illiterate

**Alternatively interesting**
  Boring git
**Alternative View Dissemination Specialist**
  London cabbie
**Aqua Technician with Bovine-Oppressive Tendencies**
  Plumber
**Attention deficit disorder**
  Liberalese for 'maladjusted little thug'


**Botanical friend**
  Houseplant
**Botanical friend conversationalist**
  Prince Charles
**BSE**
  CJD
**Bovine Oppressor**
  Cowboy


**Cerebrally deficient**
  Stupid
**Cerebrally deficient person of phallocentric polarity**
  Stupid prick
**Chronologically inexperienced client of the
correctional system**
  Young offender
**Chronologically inexperienced client of the
correctional system skilled in artistic self-expression**
  That c*nt of a young offender on day release who
  scratched his keys all down the side of your car
**Chronologically inexperienced, objectively
advantaged and melanin-enhanced**
  Young, gifted and black
**CJD**
  BSE
**Consensual rape**
  Heterosexual sex
**Conventional worldview non-possessor**
  Crank

**Cosmetically different**
Paul Daniels
**Covert tactile self-stimulation**
Crafty wank
**Cranially non-viable**
Deadhead
**Cranially associated melanin-enhanced dermatological feature**
Blackhead
**Cruelty-free products**
Products that only hurt when you see the price tag
**Culturally dispossessed, economically exploited, alternatively odoured persons of different intelligence**
The working classes
**Culturally dispossessed, economically exploited, alternatively odoured persons of different intelligence within mass domiciliary units**
Housing estates

**Differently diverse**
Specific
**Differently good**
Bad
**Differently differently good**
Good
**Differently differently differently good**
Very bad
**Differently knowledged**
Ignorant
**Differently pharmacologically preferenced**
Crackhead
**Differently visa-d guest**
Illegal immigrant
**Domiciliary deficient and non-waged**
The bums that clutter shop doorways
**Domiciliary technician**
Housewife

**Educationally non-gifted**
   Illiterate
**Educationally liberated**
   Truant
**Ergonomically designed**
   An excuse for something that looks 'cosmetically
   different' and which has an 'enhanced price point'
**Ethically different parentally deficient person**
   Lying bastard
**Experientially gifted male person of different hygiene**
   Dirty old man
**Exponents of People's Art**
   Those moronic arseholes who spray-paint
   unintelligible symbols on railway bridges and
   around housing estates
**Expressive declination of potential partner's
aesthetics**
   Don't fancy yours much!


**False consciousness**
   Everything we think we know is wrong, but only
   university professors can see through it . . .
**Familiary-rejected ovine of race**
   Black sheep of the family
**Fatefully designated, parentally deficient individual**
   Lucky bastard
**Fatefully designated, parentally deficient individual of
economic independence**
   National Lottery winner
**Female observance with verbal emotive expression**
   Ogling birds and going 'Whorrrrrr!'
**Female person of transitory status and material
self-sufficiency**
   Bag lady
**Femdarin**
   A small female orange originating from China
**Femet**
   Edouard Manet's wife

**Femifesto**
  Politically correct expression of feminist ideas
**Femufacturing**
  Self-expressing produce made by wimmin for wimmin
**Femure**
  Dung produced by female animals
**Fish rapist**
  Angler

**Heterosexual decolonisation**
  Finding Phillip Schofield attractive for the first time
**Heterosexual oppressor**
  Boyfriend
**Himpies**
  Small, painful blisters that you can get from having sex with men
**Himring**
  Intrinsically oppressive male herring

**Individual of restricted success**
  Loser
**Individual with non-traditional shopping habits**
  Shoplifter
**Intensely modified aural efficiency**
  Deaf as a post

**Leisure survivor**
  Unemployed

**Male motherhood**
  Fatherhood
**Mass Transit Executive Guidance Operative**
  Bus driver
**Melanin gifted**
  Black
**Melanin disadvantaged**
  White

**Metabolically inconvenienced**
   Dead as a doornail
**Motivationally different**
   Lazy
**Motivationally and parentally different**
   Lazy bastard

**Non-achievement achiever**
   Non-achiever
**Non-acquiescent volunteering**
   Drafting
**Non-consensual non-monogamy**
   Cheating on your wife or girlfriend
**Non-consensual gender realignment**
   What sometimes happens when you're caught
   cheating on your wife or girlfriend
**Non-consensual temporary house guest**
   Burglar
**Non-initiated wealth transferral**
   Being robbed
**Non-requested intimate physical encounter**
   Being molested
**Non-symmetrically gifted**
   Landmine victim
**Non-traditional politician**
   Honest
**Non-traditional property acquisition operative**
   Burglar
**Non-traditional property acquisition operative with
excretionary expressionistic tendencies**
   Burglar who also shits on your bed

**Ovacentric**
   From a woman's point of view
**Ovum impoverished**
   Male

**Parentally different**
   Illegitimate

266

**Parentally deficient**
Orphan
**Personal Assistant**
Jumped-up secretary
**Person of alternative sexual motivation**
A perv
**Person of different merit**
Worthless individual
**Person gifted with personality duopoly**
Schizo
**Person of moral difference**
Serial killer; pervert; chicken-strangler; politician
**Person of phallically cranial disposition**
Dickhead
**Person with antisocial tendencies of a physical nature towards his significant other**
Wife-beater
**Person with physiologically demonstrative tendencies**
Flasher
**Person with special needs**
Someone who'd be somewhere secure if they hadn't emptied all the loony-bins out into the street
**Phallically different**
Female
**Preferentially, hygienically and durationally advantaged polymer male substitute**
Vibrator
**Pre-Person's Trans-Thoroughfare Supervisory Executive**
Lollipop lady
**Preserve-resembling person of single-parent family origin**
Jammy bastard
**Profoundly aspiring carnal satisfaction**
Gagging for it
**Proletarian shopping**
Shoplifting

**Public Relief Executive Sanitation Officer**
   Bog cleaner
**Purposeful intervention in third-party metabolic cessation**
   Murder

**Reciprocated consensual temporary partner transference**
   Wife-swapping

**Sex Care Provider**
   Prostitute
**Sex Care Provider Provider**
   Pimp
**Sexual Subjugation Survivor**
   Divorcee
**Sexually insatiable with frenetic erotic responses**
   Goes like a train
**Sobriety deprived**
   Drunk
**Sobriety and gravitationally deprived**
   Falling-down drunk
**Sobriety deprived in the manner of an aquatically gifted non-mammalian animal**
   Pissed as a newt
**Sobriety deprived in the manner of a non-human smellism survivor**
   Drunk as a skunk

**Temporarily chemically inconvenienced auto operative**
   Drunk driver
**Testicularcentric**
   The man's point of view
**Thoroughfare Purification Consultant**
   Road sweeper
**Top non-achiever**
   Bottom of the class
**Truth of difference**
   A lie

**Vaginal envy**
  What men should be aware that they're really
  suffering from
**Vagina gratitude**
  The perfect antidote to penis envy
**Vendor of pharmaceutical substances for physiological enhancement**
  Drug dealer
**Vertically different, circumferentially gifted and talentially deficient**
  Little and Large
**Vicarious self-actualisation transference**
  Getting a stiffie when Big Arnie goes on a
  shoot-'em-up rampage
**Vista Decontamination Technician**
  Window cleaner

**Woman of different gender**
  Man

**And don't forget, 'Differently Sized Sibling of Male Gender' is watching you!**

**Key words to avoid when having a Politically Correct discussion**

  Black, white
  Male, female
  Right, wrong
  Good, bad
  Young, old
  Big, small
  Dead, alive
  Tall, short
  First, last
  Left, right
  Acceptable, unacceptable
  Shag

# Stiff Competition

You know how it is. You get married. Time passes. Things start to drag. You can't get it up . . .

We're both in our mid-30s now and, quite frankly, need a bit of help from you, our readers.

With this in mind, we're holding the first-ever competition to be decided entirely by erectile tissue! Yes, the winner in each category will be the entrant who succeeds in doing a Lazarus on our loins.

The categories are as follows:

## Guys

To win, all you have to do is give us an erection. That might not be as easy as it sounds – because we're 110% straight! We want you to write us the most pervie and downright politically incorrect story you can think of. One last catch – it has to feature Mariah Carey, Alanis Morissette, the girls from Abba or Suzanne Charlton.

*The prize*
This is it! The full, 100% uncensored manuscript for the book we wrote for Roy 'Chubby' Brown – *Roy Chubby Brown Unzipped!* – the one that horrified and shocked Chubby so much that it had to be *greatly* toned down for publication! Within its hundreds of deeply disturbing pages, you'll discover the previously unpublished lyrics of 'Route 69' and 'Carnival on My Nob' and will be startled by just how far a magazine mock-up entitled 'What Spunk?' can actually go!

**Girls**

What could you do to revive our flagging libidos? We want to receive your frankest ideas for turning us on. They can be physical, they can be psychological. They can even be illegal – we don't care. We just want them, nay, need them . . .

*The prize*
Naturally, no girl would ever want anything so revolting as a Chubby Brown manuscript, so we'll send you a special 'girlie' parcel full of chocs, tampons, etc. for the most arousing entrant! (Of course, if you're sick enough to win this sort of contest, you *might* like the uncensored Chubby manuscript after all. Let us know!)

You can enter as many times as you like.

We only wish that we still could.

*Send your entries to:*

DON'T TELL THEIR WIVES COMPETITION
Virgin Books
332 Ladbroke Grove
London
W10 5AH

To win, entries must be received by 31 March 1997 and don't forget to include your name and address (and if you're in the mood, a photo of yourself in a state of undress*)

* Girls only.

*Other books published by Virgin:*

## THE OFFICE REVENGE KIT

Mike Lepine and Mark Leigh

In a cruel move, following the success of *The Ultimate Revenge Kit*, Leigh and Lepine bring you a host of new, fiendish letters designed to wreak horrible revenge on all those people who have annoyed, mocked, insulted or just looked at you in an odd manner at work.

From memos detailing how everyone has to obey new working rules, to letters declaring undying love for colleagues, fake business cards from massage parlours, and telephone messages from very embarrassing places, this kit will enliven your working day no end. Or it might get you the sack, but maybe that's the point?

ISBN 0 7535 0028 0

# THE BOY RACER'S HANDBOOK

Kevin S. Court

BOY RACERS! This is funnier than a ten-point penalty. LEARNERS! You gotta read this. GRANDADS! Zimmer over to the gardening section.

At last, the definitive A–Z of hotting handbrake turns, burn-offs, furry dice, tea trays, and so much more. If you drive a Volvo, obey speed limits, think a joyride is a fairground attraction and wear zip-up slippers, this is definitely not for you.

If you wear shades at night, a baseball cap backwards, very baggy trousers and somebody else's Rolex, then snuggle up and get someone else to read this to you. From ABS (Another Bloody Safety-feature designed to render Sweeney-like stops impossible) to Zebra Crossing (if you can be bothered to stop), here is the ultimate knowledge for anyone who fancies a very swift spin in a tarted-up Cosworth Escort.

ISBN 0 7535 0023 X

## JACK DUCKWORTH:
## HOW TO LIVE THE LIFE OF RILEY

John Stevenson

Although Jack Duckworth puts a supreme amount of guile and effort into avoiding honest labour, his dodges are seldom artful. But despite his past failures, Jack is always confident that his next scam is foolproof and he's never short of bright ideas that promise a quick buck. And here's his latest ruse – a book on how to live the life of Riley, with additional helpful advice on:

WORK: how to avoid it
WOMEN: how to avoid them avoiding you
MONEY: how to get it and spend it without the wife
    finding out

With photographs and illustrations throughout, for once Jack is giving value for money.

ISBN 1 85227 681 9

# THE LIFE AND LEGACY OF REGGIE PERRIN

## A Celebration

### Richard Webber

Downtrodden suburbanite Reggie Perrin first appeared on our TV screens in 1976 in an innovative and intelligent comedy series adapted for television from his own books by David Nobbs. The first series was an immediate success and Reginald Perrin became a household name, with series two and three helping to turn Reggie, his wife, his brother-in-law, his boss and his workmates into comedy legends in a total of just ten and a half hours of on-screen adventures.

Finally, twenty years on, a fourth series, *The Legacy of Reginald Perrin*, has been completed. Published to coincide with the new series, *The Life and Legacy of Reginald Perrin* forms an essential companion, nostalgic review, light-hearted guide and, above all, an affectionate tribute to the legend of Reggie Perrin.

ISBN 1 85227 686 X

# FOOTBALL BABYLON

## Russ Williams

It's a funny old game, football. Take that centre forward who was gored to death by wild boars during a game. Or the time there were topless models in the players' bath after they'd won an important match. Cor, some players have been known to take drugs, get drunk, have punch-ups, kill referees and accept bribes. The managers can be even worse, and as for the chairmen, well, you wouldn't believe it. Would you?

Here's your chance to find out. The most astonishing, amazing, abso-bloody-lutely astounding tales of sex, death, bribery, corruption, violence and humour that you'll ever find in the game of two halves. It's a funny old game, football. Isn't it. Eh? Marvellous.

ISBN 0 7535 0046 9

# DO THAT AGAIN SON AND I'LL BREAK YOUR LEGS

## Football's Hard Men

### Phil Thompson

Football has always been a contact sport. For every gifted ball player there has always been at least one bone cruncher. There have been many players who have become infamous as soccer's hard men – Ron 'Chopper' Harris, Norman 'Bites Yer Legs' Hunter, Nobby Stiles and the infamous Tommy Smith.

*Do That Again Son and I'll Break Your Legs* is a collection of anecdotes told by the players, with comments and recollections from the game's greatest ball wizards, from Sir Stanley Matthews to George Best and Peter Beardsley. In turns chilling, humorous and amazing, this is a vivid and thrilling football compendium.

ISBN 0 7535 0002 7